Teaching Science to Culturally and Linguistically Diverse Elementary Students

Amy Cox-Petersen

California State University, Fullerton

Leah M. Melber

Lincoln Park Zoo

Terri Patchen

California State University, Fullerton

2012

Boston • Columbus • Indianapolis • New York • San Francisco • Upper Saddle River
Amsterdam • Cape Town • Dubai • London • Madrid • Milan • Munich • Paris • Montreal • Toronto
Delhi • Mexico City • Sao Paulo • Sydney • Hong Kong • Seoul • Singapore • Taipei • Tokyo

*This work is dedicated to all the birds we watched, flowers
we picked, bugs we collected, rocks we polished, and stars
we stayed up late to see . . . all of which jump-started our
careers in science education . . . and continue to inspire
learners of all cultural backgrounds as they grow
into scientifically literate adults.*

Senior Acquisitions Editor: Kelly Villella Canton
Editorial Assistant: Annalea Manalili
Marketing Manager: Danae April
Production Editor: Gregory Erb
Editorial Production Service: Element LLC
Manufacturing Buyer: Megan Cochran
Electronic Composition: Element LLC
Interior Design: Element LLC
Cover Designer: Jennifer Hart

Credits and acknowledgments borrowed from other sources and reproduced, with permission, in this textbook appear on the appropriate page within the text. Photos on pages 19, 41, 49, and 92 by Pam Cole. All other photos provided by Amy Cox-Petersen.

Cataloging-in-Publication Data not available at time of printing.

10 9 8 7 6 5 4 3 2 1   RRD-VA   15 14 13 12 11

www.pearsonhighered.com

ISBN 10: 0-13-714623-X
ISBN 13: 978-0-13-714623-9

Anne (Amy) Cox-Petersen, PhD, has more than 25 years of experience in multiple educational settings. She holds a BS in early childhood education and an MA in elementary education from East Carolina University, and a PhD in curriculum and instruction with a science education specialization from the University of Southern California. She has presented internationally and nationally on topics related to science teacher education and learning science outside the formal classroom. Her research focuses on culturally relevant science teaching and learning in classrooms, field sites, museums, and service-learning settings. She is the author of *Educational Partnerships: Connecting Schools, Families, and the Community* (Sage, 2010). She has taught in urban, suburban, and rural schools as an elementary and middle school teacher. She joined the faculty at California State University, Fullerton, in 1998 and is currently a professor in the department of elementary and bilingual education.

Photo by Angela Janas

Leah M. Melber, PhD, has 20 years of experience in informal and formal science education. She holds a BA in zoology, an MA in education, together with a multiple-subject teaching credential for the state of California, and a PhD in educational psychology from the University of Southern California. She has presented internationally on inquiry-based instruction and effective methods of connecting with cultural institutions such as museums. In addition to numerous journal articles she has written on this topic, she recently authored the book *Informal Learning and Field Trips* (Corwin Press, 2007). She was awarded the 2001 Informal Educator Award through the California Science Teachers Association, and the 2010 Promising Leadership Award from the Association of Midwest Museums. She was recently accepted as a candidate on the Fulbright Specialist Roster in the focus area of education.

Photo provided by Leah Melber

She is a former third-grade teacher and university professor in science education. She also served as the Science Education Specialist at the Natural History Museum of Los Angeles County, in addition to serving as a consultant in the area of informal education for museums around the nation. She joined the staff of Lincoln Park Zoo in December 2008, where she is currently the Director of Student and Teacher Programs.

Terri Patchen, PhD, is an associate professor in the department of elementary and bilingual education at California State University, Fullerton. A credentialed bilingual

teacher, she taught kindergarten in a lower income, Spanish-speaking classroom for close to 10 years before attaining graduate degrees in urban planning and Latin American studies, and a PhD in education from the University of California, Los Angeles. She has published in journals as diverse as *Multicultural Education* and *Science Education,* and regularly presents at education conferences. She is a lifelong advocate for the benefits of working with English learners.

Photo by Melanie Chapman

contents

Chapter **3** *Literacy Development through Science*   **34**

Chapter **6** *Family Connections*   **79**

Chapter 7   *Keeping Current and Assessing Resources*   97

This book is written for teachers who want to present science in a different way—to engage and include *all* students in understanding and doing science. We wrote this book to help K–8 teachers enact culturally relevant instructional strategies to ensure that all students, regardless of race, ethnicity, or socioeconomic class, can *do* science, *like* science, and enter science-related careers if they choose. Culturally relevant activities benefit all students, and help teachers and students alike to recognize and identify connections between science in the classroom and science in their lives. In addition, taking science outside the traditional four walls of the classroom helps to provide authentic experiences and to encourage scientific inquiry.

In America's increasingly diverse classrooms, science is not always presented in a way that is meaningful to all students. Students from non-English language backgrounds face additional challenges when learning science because of the volume of vocabulary and ways that science is presented. This text provides culturally relevant strategies for teachers to ensure that all students have access to inquiry-based, interactive, and experiential science learning.

As authors, we have decades of collective experience as classroom teachers, museum science educators, and teacher educators. We have worked in rural, urban, and suburban teaching environments with culturally and linguistically diverse students at multiple grade levels. We are excited to share our knowledge, experiences, and expertise related to teaching science to *all*.

Features

This book blends culturally relevant strategies with sound science instruction. Specific features include the following:

- *Eight overarching culturally relevant strategies:* Strategies are woven throughout the book with examples of how to implement scientifically sound, culturally relevant activities.

- *Science and literacy connections:* Examples of how you can integrate science and literacy to enhance students' understanding of science are included throughout the book.

- *Case studies:* Case studies are featured in each chapter, with reflection questions, to provide examples of culturally relevant science teaching in K–8 classrooms.
- *Book study questions:* A list of questions is provided to assist those of you who want to discuss the book professionally and apply the information learned to your current science program.
- *Science instructional models:* Specific steps to traditional models are coupled with culturally relevant examples and strategies.
- *Family connections:* Ways to encourage family involvement as partners in helping children learn science are featured throughout the book.
- *Grant funding and writing strategies:* Resources and steps are highlighted to help you obtain outside funding for science activities and programs.
- *Inquiry-based instructional strategies:* These strategies are featured throughout the book to help you assist students in asking questions, communicating with scientists, and engaging in authentic science investigations.

Acknowledgments

We are grateful for our students—at the elementary, middle school, and university levels—who have enriched our lives as educators and made this book possible.

We also thank Kelly Villella Canton, who provided guidance and support throughout the writing of the book, and Pam Cole, who took some of the photos featured within the chapters. In addition, we thank the reviewers of this text: Joe Alfano, Minneapolis Public Schools; Cheryl Harris Curtis, North Carolina Department of Public Instruction; Karisa S. Dodds, Myers Park Traditional School; Michelle Ferro, West Melbourne Elementary School for Science; Shelley White Fones, Stone Academy of Communication Arts; Craig Freeman, Hampton City Schools; Iris Green, Wellston City Schools; Ann Harris, Hillsborough Township Public Schools; Kristi Trotter Hattenhauer, Jonesboro Math and Science Magnet School; Charles H. Parsons, Douglas L. Jamerson, Jr. Elementary School; Margaret J. Secor, Salem City Schools; and Laura Wilde, Encompass Learning.

Last, we thank those special individuals who have been mentors, friends, and colleagues, and who have inspired us to teach science in a way that is fun, authentic, and accessible to all students.

Amy Cox-Petersen: I thank my students and colleagues, who continue to motivate and inspire me to be a better teacher. I also thank Dr. Floyd Mattheis, who introduced me to a different way of teaching science 23 years ago at East Carolina University and who has affected positively the field of science education for more than 50 years.

Leah Melber: I thank my many coworkers who, throughout the years, have shared their wisdom and their encouragement as we all work together to ensure quality science experiences for all learners. In particular, I thank my long-time colleagues Anne Marshall and Linda Marie, who have made my professional and personal life that much richer.

Terri Patchen: I thank my co-author, Amy Cox-Petersen, first and foremost, for bringing me into the world of science education. I also express my deepest appreciation to Alo Patchen for always reminding me that what matters most in teaching is what matters most in all good relationships: communication that is open, thoughtful, and responsive.

Why Culturally Relevant Science?

• Prior Knowledge and Beliefs Organizer •

- What does "science for all" mean to you?
- Give examples of how you currently promote "science for all" in your classroom.

Consider your responses to the questions posed above as you read through this first chapter and the rest of the book. This book is written to encourage more inclusive practices so that all students, regardless of race, ethnicity, or socioeconomic class, can *do* science, *like* science, and become scientists if they choose.

Changing Demographics

Classrooms across America keep changing. Demographic shifts in student populations in evidence 10 years ago have shifted yet again, and there is no sign of the student population stabilizing. Students are no longer just Black or White; they are increasingly also Hispanic, Asian, East Asian, South Asian, Central American, Russian, Vietnamese, African, and more. Table 1.1 presents data from the Forum on Child and Family Statistics (2006) that indicate that children in the United States come from a variety of ethnic and racial backgrounds. In addition, 21% of children live with at least one foreign-born parent, and 19% of children live with families who speak languages other than English at home. Compared with 10 years ago, children today are far more likely to come from

TABLE 1.1   Children in the United States

Percentage of Children Ages 0–17 Years	Ethnicity/Racial Identity
58.9	White (non-Hispanic)
19.2	Hispanic
15.5	Black
3.9	Asian
4.1	All other races

Source: Forum on Child and Family Statistics (2006).

working-class families, to have two parents of the same gender, to be homeless, to be nonnative English speakers, or to have some identified disability. Yet even as classrooms across the United States grow increasingly diverse, not all subject areas are taught in ways that consider or respond to this diversity.

Teaching Science with Access for All Students

In America's increasingly diverse classrooms, science is not always presented in a way that is meaningful to all students. All teachers need to help ensure that our students are able to access and understand what we teach, and this is particularly true with regard to science. Remember when you first encountered science in school? If you were lucky, your teacher introduced you to science through some hands-on or inquiry-based instruction. Perhaps you watched the wonder of metamorphosis from larvae to butterflies. If you weren't so lucky and were in one of the more traditional classrooms, you opened up a textbook and kept it open for the rest of the year. For those of us familiar with the day-to-day practices of U.S. classrooms, the predominant mode of textbook-focused instruction left us disinterested and unenthusiastic about science. For students unfamiliar with U.S. instruction, however, depending primarily upon textbooks to teach science locks them out completely.

Children inquire about the natural world around them.

Challenges for Students from Non-English Language Backgrounds

It is important to note that students from non-English language backgrounds face additional challenges when learning science because of the volume of vocabulary and ways that science is presented. Textbooks often include complex sentence structures, vocabulary, and activities with multiple steps and confusing directions. When we use the textbook as the sole or primary guide for science instruction, students are expected to do a great amount of reading. In this way, rather than engaging in a process that involves students in learning actual science concepts and skills, science instruction turns into reading instruction. Rivet and Krajcik (2008) reported that science instruction delivered in this manner is not contextualized and does not relate to students' prior knowledge and experiences. To make science more meaningful, it is important to access students' prior understanding of science topics, encourage native language connections to vocabulary, and implement interactive activities that allow students to "experience" science.

The purpose of this book, therefore, is to provide information, strategies, and sample lessons to promote access to science for all students, particularly those students from culturally, linguistically, and academically diverse backgrounds. We refer to these strategies as *culturally relevant teaching* or *instruction*.

What Is Culturally Relevant Teaching?

Some researchers have argued that learning science is like crossing a border, because the language, methods, and content in science are different from what ethnic minority or lower socioeconomic status children experience in the home (see, for example, Aikenhead and Jegede [1999]). Access to science for everyone can be like moving across an unseen and unknown dividing line into another world—one where some students do not understand what is being said or why things are being done. A culturally relevant science program, however, helps students navigate across and beyond this border which has traditionally kept many students out.

Culturally relevant teaching helps teachers better support the introduction and instruction of science for all students. Culturally relevant instruction not only teaches by doing (like the metamorphosis example given earlier), but it also teaches to and through students' experiences, connecting science activities and content to students' lives at home.

Here are some terms that will help you think about culture and the celebration and acceptance of diverse cultures and views in the science classroom:

- **Culture:** Behaviors exhibited by individuals or a group of people, including how they communicate, the languages they speak, gender roles and responsibilities, where and how they live, the foods they eat, moral and ethical beliefs, and their hobbies, music, and/or other activities.

- **Assimilation:** A subtractive process that requires students and families to abandon their ethnic backgrounds and beliefs (eliminating anything that might make them *different*) and to adopt the dominant culture. (Assimilation, although supportive of some elements of integration, usually results in the loss of ethnic identification and self-worth.)

- **Pluralism:** An additive process based on the mutual respect of distinct cultures; allows for individual and cultural expression as long as this expression does not disrupt social harmony or the survival of the society as a whole (Bennett, 2007).

In this book, we value pluralism as a more culturally relevant strategy when working with students and families, because pluralism recognizes that differences exist among cultures and peoples; it supports the mutual respect of individuals and their integration into society.

Gloria Ladson-Billings (1995), one of the leaders in developing culturally relevant teaching, is known for a communal approach to instruction that recognizes the individual humanity, capacity, and worth of all students. She advocates better balancing of authority in the classroom so that teachers and students learn from one another. According to Ladson-Billings, culturally relevant teaching encompasses:

- **Assisting all students** to achieve academic success

- **Focusing on cultural competence** to help students maintain their own cultural integrity through classroom activities

- **Ensuring critical consciousness** through activities that address cultural norms, values, and social inequities

What Does Culturally Relevant Science Instruction Look Like?

We use Ladson-Billings' view (1995) of culturally relevant instruction as a springboard to describe what culturally relevant teaching looks like in the science classroom. A traditional view of a "variety of teaching methods" usually includes visuals, hands-on activities, cooperative learning, and experiments—all valuable instructional tools. However, to begin thinking about culturally relevant practices requires the design and use of *explicit* strategies to encourage all students to consider themselves successful in science. Such strategies include the following and are based in part on the research of Patchen and Cox-Petersen (2008):

- **Promoting inquiry-based instruction:** Engaging students in science experiments, collecting and examining data, and asking authentic questions

- **Diversifying seating and grouping:** Establishing opportunities for students to work individually, in dyads, and cooperatively in small groups

- **Connecting to students' lives at home:** Linking science practices in the classroom with students' home lives and everyday experiences; reconceptualizing *home*work

- **Creating a shared learning environment:** Shifting authority so that students take more responsibility in science activities and their own learning

- **Redistributing authority and redefining classroom responsibilities:** Redesigning and redistributing classroom practices so that students and teachers share in decision making about content and activities

- **Encouraging real, active, and engaged conversations:** Building on students' knowledge and experiences in the development of meaningful science conversations

- **Creating a safe environment:** Ensuring student and teacher responses are highly valued and listened to

- **Developing students' capacity to think and act independently:** Scaffolding students' understanding of science through activities that build self-confidence, develop competence, and motivate learning in science

Let's look at each of these strategies to see how you can use them in the practice of culturally relevant science instruction.

Promoting Inquiry-Based Instruction

In many classrooms, teachers use a variety of valuable instructional strategies to teach science, such as visuals, hands-on objects, cooperative learning groups, and controlled experiments. Yet, unless students are supported in connecting their prior experiences to these often new and unfamiliar strategies, science content knowledge will remain exclusive to a select group of students. Moving toward culturally relevant instruction, therefore, depends on teachers supporting these connections. You can do this by creating activities that include and build on students' experiences, questions, and self-designed procedures to solve science problems. Culturally relevant science instruction also means that you shift from using direct instruction only and begin to provide more inquiry-based instruction, more student-led discussion and exploration, and more opportunities for transferences of authority (and not just knowledge) between you and your students. During the process of cultivating these types of shifts, students can

- Use prior knowledge to connect science content to their lived experiences outside of school and larger social processes *beyond* home and school

- Extend relationships and science activities beyond the classroom

- Engage in positive attitudes related to science, science careers, and learning science

Diversifying Seating and Grouping

Seating students in the classroom is a fundamental issue for most teachers. Teachers often determine a seating chart and then stick to it, moving students only if they are bothering others or behaving inappropriately in some way. It is the rare classroom, indeed, where teachers shift seating randomly or regularly, so if you do this, consider yourself on the leading edge!

How such movement becomes *radical* is apparent when you think about how easy it becomes not to *see* those students who occupy the same seat all year long. We have found that moving students around the classroom—in and out of their chairs, in and of groups with others—results in increased contacts, opportunities, and interactions with others. The very focus on shifting results in a change of perspective, a willingness to consider what was not there before, to listen to different ideas, to hear different voices, and to ponder different understandings: all of which are important variables in developing inter-cultural competence. Shifting seating also applies to the ways in which students move through the day: as a whole class, in small groups, with partners, and alone. Ensuring that students have the opportunity to work with different students in different ways, results in more cross-cultural interaction. Each distinct seating possibility holds the promise of elucidating a new way of sharing and understanding—two key elements in accessing science. Specific ways to diversify grouping include the following:

- Extend classroom activities. Use contexts outside the four walls of the classroom to help students connect science outside of class with curriculum content. Pair students with those they haven't worked with much before to investigate things in and on the school grounds.

- Ensure groups are heterogeneous, and not just based upon academic ability. Mix students from different linguistic, social, gender, and ethnic groups.

- Provide activities in and out of chairs, and in and out of groups with others during science activities. Set up whole class projects that require students to work in small groups to piece together parts of a larger, complete whole.

- Provide cooperative group work to inquire about scientific phenomena in flexible groups that change over time. Clearly identify roles in the groups and ensure students rotate through these roles. Make sure your English language learners (ELLs) are not *always* the "recorders" or "artists" for the groups; distribute leadership responsibilities equitably.

Connecting to Students' Lives at Home

FAMILY
CONNECTIONS

Delgado-Gaitan (2004) recommends three important conditions that lead to more family participation:

1. Sharing information with families
2. Connecting to the different families
3. Supporting their continued involvement

Every family offers tremendous resources from which you can learn and use to enhance science lessons. Listening to students and their families provides information about what students understand and what they have to offer. Also, communicating with families and students on a regular basis helps in constructing a shared understanding of classroom events.

One way to start the dialogue is by taking the initiative to find out more about students and their families through a class- or student-created survey to send home. In the survey, ask families to complete information related to their favorite events, foods, customs, hobbies, movies, books, or music, along with science experiences they had during their formal schooling or during informal experiences in their communities. Use pictures next to key concepts to help families less fluent in English understand (for example, include a picture of a rice bowl, a pot, or a skillet to symbolize foods eaten). These images will also help families from non-English language backgrounds communicate about these things with their families. Students can then interview their families and report the information back to their classmates. Students can also invite a member of their family to come to school to discuss specific elements from the survey (such as things they do as a family, household responsibilities, favorite cultural traditions, or celebrations).

Example 1.1 shows a sample survey that a third-grade teacher created with his students and sent out to parents. Parents were asked to complete the open-ended survey

EXAMPLE 1.1 Sample Family Survey

- Describe your favorite indoor and outdoor family activities. (*This included a picture of a house, and an image of a patio with a tree and a lake in the background.*)
- What is one of your favorite movies or favorite books? List them here. (*This included a picture of a movie reel and a book.*)
- List your favorite songs or music. (*This was accompanied by musical notes and a radio.*)
- List your child's greatest strengths. (*This showed a picture of a child smiling.*)
- List things that your child struggles with. (*This had an image of a child looking frustrated and numbers/math written around him.*)
- What is most interesting to your child about science? (*This had a child with a picture of different types of snakes.*)
- What would you like me to know about your child? (*This ended with a big question mark, a happy child's face, and a smiling teacher.*)

with their children to promote better communication, understanding, and empowerment. Responses can be in written or visual form. This is not supposed to be a "secret" activity, but a way to encourage three-way communication among families, students, and the teacher. Integrating students' strengths and interests into science lessons creates acceptance and appreciation of students' cultural and individual identities. Some teachers use the survey information to incorporate students' favorite music, books, and even pop culture into subsequent science lessons. This shows students and their families that the way they live fits in with the way they learn.

With each science endeavor that occurs in class, you can establish connections and prompt inquiry for students to develop outside of class, with their families. Ensuring instruction is relevant means building on what students know, and using their experiences and understandings to scaffold, or develop, knowledge related to science. After students are introduced to basic concepts in class—inquiry, forming hypotheses, testing, analyzing, and reporting—you can then ask students to analyze how science is incorporated into their everyday lives. Some educators recommend that families tell stories and create cultural memoirs (see Allen [2007] for more information). These projects can be accomplished in native languages to enhance multicultural and multilingual benefits, and can relate to family science experiences.

Rethinking Homework Assignments Jianzhong (2005) found that consistent completion of homework resulted in approval from teachers, peers, and families, and good discipline behaviors for middle school and high school students. However, some homework assignments take too much time, are too repetitive, and can cause undue strain on families and students, particularly for those students who are not yet fluent in English. Rethinking homework is important because researchers have shown that many homework assignments are nothing more than busywork (see, for example, Bennett and Kalish [2006] and Kohn [2006]). Yet for students struggling with developing fluency in English, busywork that is heavily dependent on English literacy may mean these students are missing out on family interactions, physical exercise, or the development of social skills through play in order to complete incomprehensible and often irrelevant homework tasks.

FAMILY CONNECTIONS

Some researchers (see Cooper [1994], for example) recommend that teachers and families consider the 10-minute rule when assigning homework. For children in first grade, this means homework should take no more than 10 minutes; in second grade, 20 minutes; third grade, 30 minutes; and so on. Given this

---

SIDEBAR 1.1
Science at Home

Children can enhance their understanding of science while at home. One way to support these connections is for you to send home a monthly newsletter that asks families to choose specific assignments and activities to complete together. These can include activities such as free museum Sundays, nature hikes, cooking with science, and problem-solving games. This creates a shared educational experience for the entire family.

formula (and assuming a general focus on mathematics and language arts), there is usually little time for science homework, and what many teachers fear even more: *no time for good and engaging* science homework. It is important, therefore, for you to provide meaningful homework experiences that build on students' background knowledge and connect learning at school to learning at home. In addition, integrating science homework activities with literacy and math assignments when possible will facilitate science communication in the home. Sample science homework assignments are presented in Example 1.2.

EXAMPLE 1.2 Sample Alternative Science Homework Assignments

Grade Level	Sample Homework Assignments
K–2	• Bring home a class animal or other interesting object. Write a story that describes the animal or object. • Plant a seed (and let students decide what type of seed!), water it, record observations each day, and measure growth and changes on individual and class charts. • Observe the moon on a daily basis. On a blank calendar, record the moon phase and what time it was seen. Look for patterns during the course of the month. Write about the patterns.
3–5	• Take a walk to a local park, in the backyard, or in a vacant lot. Observe what lives there (for example, ants, spiders, pill bugs, slugs, worms, birds, and squirrels). Draw and write about what is seen, and include animal structures, habitat, and behaviors. • Take a walk around the neighborhood and count the number of steps you take and the number of steps other family members take. Draw a map of your route, record each person's steps in a graph, and then compute the average number of steps taken by all. • Create a collection of rocks, leaves, or other objects outside or in the home. Classify these objects into different groups. Write about why you classified them in this way.
6–8	• Choose a type of food in your home that has a nutrition label on the container. Calculate the percentage of fats, protein, and other nutrients. Create a pie chart that shows this information and explain whether it is a food that should be eaten for breakfast, lunch, or dinner. • Choose an area of observation in your neighborhood with a family member or friend. Observe the animals that you see. Discuss the living and nonliving interactions taking place.

Creating a Shared Learning Environment

One teacher and many students usually occupy the classroom. By creating a shared learning environment in which students take more responsibility in science activities and their own learning, students realize they have a role in their instruction, and they can influence what and how they study. This is often referred to as *shared decision making* or *the redistribution of authority* during science instruction. Shifting responsibilities and asking students where the class might look next to deepen understanding of particular science topics, helps students better understand systematic power relations in the classroom and in their communities or homes. In addition, sharing authority means restructuring relationships, as students and teachers work together to scaffold and build instruction to make it more explicit, meaningful, and comprehensible to all students.

Indeed, the most satisfying element of increasing more students' access to science appears in the development of relationships in the classroom. It is in this most fundamental of classroom dimensions that we find the most successes and the most accessible advances; and it is here that real shifts in authority can occur, as you welcome and develop student interests in science.

What is most important in establishing relationships via culturally relevant instruction, therefore, is to move beyond sharing your life and structure to sharing and recognition of your students' lives. To communicate significantly with students, you must foster real, active, and engaged conversations—conversations in which content and expression matter, students and teacher alike are listened to, and thoughts are formed, modified, and reshaped. This will work to bolster not only student participation, but also the establishment of relationships between students and the teacher, and between the students themselves, which will serve to cultivate relationships on other levels.

For this to happen on any substantive scale, you must acknowledge and integrate the cultures of your students as well as your own. Absent this inclusion of student cultures, it becomes that much more difficult to establish real relationships, to connect classrooms to larger processes outside classrooms (economic, political, or social processes), and to shift authority to students. A key way to overcome the tendency to neglect student experiences is to provide lots of opportunities for communication, to ask lots of "authentic" questions (such as contextualized, open-ended, or connecting) about science, and to have students bring in things, people, or information from home.

Last, to make the move to culturally relevant instruction, you need to ensure independence is structured into classroom relationships. Identifying and developing students' capacity to think and act independently establishes the foundation necessary to make the shift toward culturally relevant instruction. When shared authority is a consistent classroom practice, what emerges over time is a cultural model in which all students have access to science.

Redistributing Authority and Redefining Classroom Responsibilities

A culturally relevant classroom is a place where students and teachers share in decision making about content and activities. Teachers and students can work toward creating diverse responsibilities that encourage shared authority. In many classrooms, teachers use "monitors" of one form or another. Some teachers have pencil, door, or bathroom monitors, whereas others have pushed the construct into ever more integrated roles that include establishing content monitors (who are in charge of looking up/confirming science information, sending e-mail to science experts, and so forth), production assistants (who help in the "production" of the classroom by taking care of structural issues: distribution, task leaders, reporters), and classroom critics (who collect and analyze student feedback on classroom practices and science activities). The adoption of any one of these roles results in shifts in the location of authority in the classroom, which can then be used to bolster students' self- and social awareness. As more roles and responsibilities are introduced, recognized, and valued in the classroom, you will bring students ever closer to understanding power, shifting control, and a redistribution of authority.

Adopting a diversified group of monitors diminishes the "policing" or "tracking" dimensions of what many teachers do, and it does so through a mere elaboration of what many teachers already do (adopting monitors in class). Moreover, by integrating students into the running of a classroom, the production of additional shifts in authority—from teacher-determined to student-determined foci for study, or from teacher-selected to student-selected emphases of study, for example—becomes that much easier. Classrooms can then reflect more closely some of the most basic tenets of culturally relevant science instruction. Supporting student engagement and the development of individual student authority and understanding in science can be enhanced by

- Integrating students into the running of a classroom, and helping to establish tasks and procedures related to developing science questions and finding answers
- Using classroom participation and shared decision making to redistribute authority *through* interaction in the classroom

Encouraging Real, Active, and Engaged Conversations

Authentic conversations in the classroom include active participation and listening by the students and the teacher. Social interdependence and language are integral parts of students' cultures in schools. When you deepen your responsiveness to your students as individuals, listening and speaking to them in respectful ways, you are saying that each student matters. This may sound simple, but it meets a primary need in all of us—and one that is often given short shrift in these fast-paced times. Yet its importance cannot be overstated, particularly for those students too often neglected from more mainstream, middle-class opportunities; not all students know that they *do* matter. Fostering real, active, and engaged conversations about science continuously refines students' power to speak, to hear, and to be heard, all of which are key elements in developing knowledge and understanding, and in being recognized as someone who matters, someone with something to say. In this environment, content and expression are respected. You can help students as they think about power in science and science content. Some activities include the following:

- Have students use multiple texts, resources, and materials when determining science content. Not all science is portrayed the same in each source. Questioning sources of knowledge and inquiring further help students become more empowered when learning about science.
- Encourage participation in some form from all students. Allow them to make contributions to small-group discussions if they feel uncomfortable in larger groups. Allow beginning ELLs to draw instead of writing.
- Focus on a balance between teacher talk and student talk. Support students' capacity to ask questions and direct conversations.
- Extend relationships *beyond* the classroom to include families and the broader community. Bring family members into the classroom to talk about their experiences with science.

Creating a Safe Environment and Developing Students' Capacity to Think and Act Independently

Creating a safe environment includes more than just physical safety. Here, we are referring more specifically to emotional and social safety—a place where student and teacher responses, ideas, and beliefs are valued and listened to. Science can be scary, both in terms of what we know about it and certainly in terms of all we do *not* know. However, culturally relevant teachers can support students through these new and unfamiliar experiences by discussing the mysteries of metacognitive processes as they move through science projects, engaging in self-reflection (then asking the students to do so), and requesting feedback to develop better practices. Ensuring the classroom is a safe place by first *showing* the students that there are plenty of things we do not know helps deepen and expand students' capacity to think, act independently, take initiative, and develop their confidence in science.

Some activities that establish a safe environment for learning while encouraging critical thinking and reflection include the following:

- Have students provide their own views and connections related to science content on a large bulletin board that changes and is updated as students' understanding of science concepts is enhanced.

- Encourage discourse about science topics of students' choice with appreciation of students' native language and experiences.

- Eat lunch with different groups of students one day each week to form more mutually respectful relationships.

- Use students' own ideas and labels in addition to their native language to encourage greater comprehension and connection to science concepts.

- Incorporate science assessment that goes beyond paper-and-pencil tests to include concept maps, drawings, interviews, projects, and portfolios.

- Ask questions and share strategies about how to answer questions, as well as how to ask them.

A teacher assists students with observation of leaves.

The Book You Hold in Your Hands

The book you hold in your hands is an in-depth examination of the daily practice and techniques of culturally relevant science instruction. In this first chapter, we have examined why you should consider teaching science with a culturally relevant focus, and what culturally relevant science instruction looks like.

Chapter 2 explores culturally relevant inquiry and action—two key components in the teaching of a science practice. Chapter 3 argues for an integration of science instruction and literacy, along with other subjects and skills across the disciplines. A range of teaching strategies that promote science access for all students is the subject of Chapter 4, whereas Chapter 5 deals with methods related to the accurate assessment and evaluation of culturally and linguistically diverse science students. Chapter 6 recognizes and examines the importance of family and community in the science classroom, whereas identifying resources and current instructional support is the subject of Chapter 7. Each chapter offers valuable hints for classroom topics and activities, balancing theory with concrete and readily accessible ideas for classroom projects, strategies, and goals. Each chapter also begins and concludes with a set of questions that is meant to prompt the sort of instructor inquiry and self-reflection that results in a vibrant and culturally relevant science classroom.

Culturally relevant science instruction goes beyond "good teaching" and acknowledges the gaps between what teachers often expect or believe and what students know or hope for. We like to think of the book you hold in your hands as an essential sourcebook for culturally relevant science instruction, a resource to help make science instruction accessible and exciting to an increasingly diverse student body, and to inspire America's next generation of young scientists and researchers. Culturally relevant instruction supports teaching so that every student can do science (and maybe enter a career in science one day)! In other words, culturally relevant science instruction is essential to our future.

CASE STUDY   Snapshot of a Culturally Relevant Classroom

This case study features Ahna, a third-grade teacher who uses the eight culturally relevant strategies just presented to teach students about plant and animal life in a desert environment. Ahna brings her third-grade students outside and asks them to find a place to sit on one of the school's picnic benches for their science lesson. She begins by asking them to share what they know about different types of biomes. Students are eager to talk, but not about the topic at hand.

It's September in East Los Angeles and the temperature is approaching 80 degrees. Rather than share their understanding of different habitats, students are grumbling about their discomfort. Some complain they are starting to sweat, others find the plastic bench seats are so hot they can't sit on them comfortably while wearing their shorts and light cotton skirts. Just before students lose complete focus, Ahna poses a critical question: "Does this remind you of any particular type of habitat?"

It doesn't take long for students to respond in chorus, "*A desert!*" Their attention is immediately refocused on their teacher.

Ahna smiles and asks them to think about how they might make themselves more comfortable. Rather than asking for raised hands, she encourages them to talk to a neighbor first about their ideas. This encourages even the shyest of students to share their views, and allows for students to communicate in their primary language if they choose. After providing several minutes for these discussions, she asks students to share some of the ideas they heard from their neighbors. This opportunity for students to hear their peers speak positively about their ideas can be a critical confidence builder.

"Juan said we should move to those benches over there in the shade."

"Katie said she would stay here if we were allowed to bring our bottles of water."

"Tin told me if we were going to meet outside more often he was going to start wearing shorts rather than long pants."

Ahna asks students to think about some of the ideas they just heard and to think back to their lesson on animal adaptations from last week. She poses the question, "Do any of your suggestions sound like things a desert animal might rely on for survival?"

Students immediately start chatting excitedly to their neighbors about tortoises that burrow underground and succulent plants that can store water for survival during dry times of the year. Ahna then asks them to think about how being hot and uncomfortable—even for a short time—might help them better understand the importance of adaptation for an animal's survival. As the students chat excitedly, Ahna leads them to the shady part of the schoolyard. She wants them to be cool and comfortable when they all discuss these concepts in more detail.

Reflecting on the Case

1. What aspects of culturally relevant instruction did Ahna incorporate in her lesson?

2. How were students empowered to speak and participate?

3. How did Ahna motivate and assist students in understanding the science content?

• Book Study Questions •

1. How is your culture reflected in your instruction? What aspects of your teaching style reflect how you learned?

2. What do you find the most interesting about other cultures?

3. Which of the culturally relevant strategies identified in this chapter do you already use?

4. Which strategy would you like to use more often?

5. How do you share authority with your students?

6. What concerns you most about using more culturally relevant instruction?

• References and Suggested Readings •

Aikenhead, G. S., & Jegede, O. J. (1999). Cross-cultural science education: A cognitive explanation of a cultural phenomenon. *Journal of Research in Science Teaching, 36,* 269–287.

Allen, J. (2007). *Creating welcoming schools: A practical guide to home-school partnerships with diverse families.* New York: Teachers College Press.

Bennett, C. (2007). *Comprehensive multicultural education: Theory and practice.* 6th ed. Boston: Allyn & Bacon.

Bennett, S., & Kalish, N. (2007). *The case against homework: How homework is hurting children and what parents can do about it.* New York: Three Rivers Press.

Bennett, S., & Kohn, A. (2006). *The case against homework.* New York: Crown.

Cooper, H. (1994). *The battle over homework.* Newbury Park, CA: Corwin.

Delgado-Gaitan, C. (2004). *Involving Latino families in schools: Raising student achievement through home-school partnerships.* Thousand Oaks, CA: Corwin.

Forum on Child and Family Statistics (2006). *America's children in brief: Key national indicators of well-being.* Washington, DC: Federal Interagency on Child and Family Statistics.

Kohn, A. (2006). *The homework myth: Why our kids get too much of a bad thing.* Cambridge, MA: Da Capo Press.

Jianzhong, X. (2005). Purposes for doing homework reported by middle and high school students. *Journal of Educational Research*, 99, 46.

Ladson-Billings, G. (1995). But that's just good teaching! The case for culturally relevant pedagogy. *Theory into Practice 34*, 159–165.

Patchen, T., & Cox-Petersen, A. (2008). Constructing cultural relevance in science: A case study of two elementary teachers. *Science Education, 92,* 994–1014.

Rivet, A. E., & Krajcik, J. S. (2008). Conceptualizing instruction: Leveraging students' prior knowledge and experiences to foster understanding of middle school science. *Journal of Research in Science Teaching, 45,* 79–100.

Culturally Relevant Inquiry and Action

• Prior Knowledge and Beliefs Organizer •

- Describe what science is and what scientists do.
- Describe your experiences with scientists (currently and when you were younger).

Consider your responses to the questions posed above as you read about scientific methods, activities, and strategies that benefit all students.

Scientific Methods and Processes

To prepare students for a lifetime of science literacy, school science programs should be as similar to the true work of scientists as possible. Thus, we must look at what scientists do to help determine how we teach. First and foremost, scientists study the world around them through the process of scientific inquiry. Scientific inquiry is the systematic process of planning investigations, collecting and analyzing data around a central concern, and proposing answers and explanations based on this research (National Research Council, 1996). All science moves through these processes, but that does not mean there is only one way to do science. Instead, scientists tailor their methodologies to create the best match to the topic being studied. For example, many of us were taught to follow *the* scientific method, starting with a hypothesis and ending with a result that either proved or disproved said hypothesis. This type of investigation is certainly fundamental to science, but it is not the *only* method. To understand the work of scientists, therefore, it is important to begin by acknowledging the many pathways that scientific investigation can take.

Misconceptions about scientists and the work they do are prevalent in our society, and they begin with the way we *see* scientists. For many students, science looks like this: a lone man in a lab coat, brow knit in concentration, leaning over a beaker, and scratching letters, numbers, and symbols on a piece of paper (van Eijck & Roth, 2008). However, to those familiar with the world of science, this image is a far cry from reality; science is a community effort in which male and female scientists work together in the process of "doing" science (Ford, 2008).

These types of misconceptions must be addressed and corrected to help students see that they, too, can be scientists. The first step in making any changes to outdated notions lies in determining the specific misconceptions students have about scientists and scientific work. One way to get at students' ideas and perceptions about scientists is to administer a version of the Draw-a-Scientist Test (DAST) (see, for example, Mason et al. [1991] and Barman [1999]). By asking students to represent their perceptions with a visual drawing of a scientist, the DAST allows teachers to tap into images students have about scientists. The benefits of this strategy are twofold. First, for students who speak English and are familiar with general school codes and processes, the DAST illustrates whether such familiarity and awareness extends to science. Second, for ethnic minorities and ELLs less familiar with school codes, the DAST illustrates what they understand about scientists in a way that is not dependent on academic language or writing. The following steps describe how you can incorporate this strategy into your classroom:

- **Draw and write:** Ask students to draw a picture of scientist at work, then write (or dictate) a sentence or two that describes their picture.
- **Review the drawings and writings:** Discuss student drawings in small groups and with the whole class to determine what your students already know about scientists and what they do. To bring student images of scientists into contact with their experiences, extend discussions on scientists by asking students where their drawn scientist lives, what their scientist likes to eat, and what their scientist likes to do when work is over for the day.
- **Determine patterns and take action:** Review all the student drawings to identify prevalent themes and to address stereotypes or misconceptions in subsequent classroom instruction and activities. For example, if the majority of students draw a scientist conducting a chemistry experiment, expose students to other types of scientific investigations, such as zoologists observing wolf migrations and pack patterns, astronomers peering at far-off galaxies through a telescope, paleontologists studying fossils of shells that they found in the mountains, or oceanographers studying fish populations to determine the effects of global warming. Also, if the majority of

students draw male scientists, it is important to incorporate examples of female scientists and researchers into classroom study regularly and consistently.

Children's drawings of scientists.

- **Provide examples of diverse scientists and their research:** Provide materials related to the work of scientists from diverse backgrounds (such as newspaper articles, pictures of ethnically diverse scientists and their work, video and/or film clips of scientists in action) to expose students to the different methods and practices that constitute the full field of science, and to increase all students' understanding of the cultural diversity present among practicing scientists. Consistently acknowledge that all types of people from all over the world "do" science.

Inquiry Process Skills

The national standards remind us that hands-on experiences for students are not sufficient for developing true science literacy. Rather, they advocate for "minds-on" science in conjunction with hands-on exploration of concepts to support student learning (National Research Council, 1996). We call this type of learning *inquiry*. Inquiry allows all students to take more responsibility for their own learning as they ask science-related questions, to determine ways of answering the questions (while distinguishing between who holds the power of knowledge), and to interpret findings. Utilizing inquiry in the classroom is especially helpful for ELLs, because it is based in active investigation experiences that not only expand science content by providing critical context, but also support developing English fluency in context-heavy and engaging ways (Dobb, 2004). Inquiry allows all students to take more responsibility for their own learning because they

- Ask science-related questions
- Determine ways to answer the questions
- Interpret findings

- Make the decisions
- Communicate results
- Become scientists during the process!

Although science educators and researchers are in agreement that there is not a single method to conducting scientific investigations, there is agreement on a set of inquiry process skills that are relied on regularly when conducting research. The national standards outline key process skills critical to conducting inquiry-based activities and investigations. These inquiry skills are not a laundry list of steps to be followed in sequence, however. They represent a range of skills to develop in students so they will become careful and attentive researchers. The following is a list of the process skills of science and strategies to make these process skills more culturally relevant.

> ### ⌕ SIDEBAR 2.1
> **Inquiry Process Skills**
>
> Making observations
>
> Posing questions
>
> Examining information sources
>
> Planning investigations
>
> Using tools to gather, analyze, and interpret data
>
> Making predictions and proposing explanations
>
> Communicating results
>
> *Source:* National Research Council (1996, p. 23).

Making Observations

Students are naturally curious about their world; yet, in this age of electronics and quick information, students often need extra instruction on how to conduct slow, careful observations. This means that opportunities for observations need to be engaging, to attract and hold students' interest, and to result in real observable changes—whether visual, audible, tactile, olfactory, or taste based. Build on students' experiences in setting up observational activities, and model careful observation for students. Scaffold student experiences by asking relevant and open-ended questions related to what they already know that requires them to look more carefully or to determine why something is happening. Move beyond visual observations and encourage students to use their other senses to take in information that builds on their own experiences or understanding. Encouraging the development of careful observation skills not only supports science learning, but also increases attentiveness in other areas of the curriculum.

Children observe changes in plants over time.

Posing Questions

When referring to inquiry-based learning, the process of questioning should originate with the student, rather than the teacher, whenever possible. Initially, it may be difficult for some students to take this role (and this may be a culturally determined element), but through teacher modeling of how to ask a variety of questions, students will develop the capacity to ask and respond to questions that tap into different skills, such as description, analysis, or synthesis. As students take part in engaging in relevant science activities, they will naturally identify areas of further interest, especially when activities build on their prior knowledge and interests. If you cannot answer all their questions "in the moment," keep a running list that you refer to on a daily or weekly basis and answer these questions as a class activity whenever possible. Encouraging this process not only models the work of practicing scientists, but also validates students' understanding and increases intrinsic motivation for further study in other scientific areas.

Examining Information Sources

A great deal of scientific discovery has already taken place, so encourage students to investigate what scientists know and what they don't know. This is a way to build on previous studies and findings, and it is something that we all do. Regardless of whether we are researching best practices for teaching, developing new activities, or searching for new materials to use in our classes, we look to see what has already been done. It is important, too, to remember to avoid the pitfall of simply reading a textbook for answers; the textbook is but one resource. Use a variety of sources to nurture inquiry-based learning, critical thinking, and more culturally relevant practices.

Provide students with information sources in line with what a practicing scientist might use. These might include relevant websites, informational texts aligned to students' reading and interest levels, video resources, or even connections to experts through e-mail or guest presentations. The multiple sources and resources (1) provide tools that help students distinguish between the different forms of disciplinary authority (i.e., *how science is presented* in different ways within text materials and Internet sites), and (2) expose students to distinct sources, philosophies, and ways of learning and thinking. You are far more likely to connect with a child, to inspire a child, and to support a child's comprehension by providing a variety of materials than you are by relying on one or two state-adopted texts. In science, new knowledge is gained by using resources and tools.

Planning Investigations

Children will naturally want to try new things and test out their ideas. It's important to support the process of planning an investigation to encourage student-generated questions and interest. Investigations do not need to be lengthy, elaborate, or consist of a multitude of materials to be effective. Some of the most important discoveries in science were narrowly focused, attentive to one thing, and took place over time and at the scientist's pace (consider Galileo!). Many students plan investigations when they stomp on a ketchup packet, throw a wad of paper towel at the bathroom ceiling to see if (or how long) it sticks, or find out whether school scissors can cut human hair. Harnessing these investigative desires into safe and student-relevant, standard-based experiences is an important step in creating an inquiry-based curriculum that is also culturally relevant.

Using Tools to Gather, Analyze, and Interpret Data

In inquiry-based science, the focus is on students collecting their own data and making sense of what they have collected. Sometimes the data will be quantitative, such as how long it takes an ice cube to melt or how much an apple weighs. Other times, data will be qualitative or narrative, such as the description of two types of leaves, or mealworm behavior over time. Even very young children can collect and record data. When a kindergarten student notices the weather outside and hangs the appropriate icon on the classroom calendar, that's an example of collecting data. Older students may take part in more advanced methods, such as recording plant growth or daily temperatures. Allowing students to use appropriate scientific tools, such as thermometers, rulers, and magnifying glasses, further replicates the work of scientific researchers. After the data have been gathered, students should be guided on interpreting the information they have collected. Are temperatures getting hotter or cooler over time? Are all the descriptions of the leaves the same? What happens to fish when it's doused in lemon juice? Is the traditional Mexican dish *ceviche* "cooked" during this process?

Children look for living organisms under leaves.

Making Predictions and Proposing Explanations

Inquiry-based science requires that students use hands-on explorations and information gathering not only to learn new information but also to determine further areas of study. After data have been gathered, it is important to provide students with the opportunity to explain their results and answer the original questions with which they initiated their investigation. These are key tenets of all research. Sometimes students will make predictions prior to beginning their investigation. Other times, open-ended investigations will lead students to a prediction that requires more focused testing and exploration. In either situation, it is important to revisit what prompted the study and how the data collected responds to those initial steps or questions. Proposing explanations, establishing certain conditions, making predictions, and tracking changes are all important to developing understanding of science. Avoid use of the word *guess*; this will help orient students to the relationships that exist between thoughtful questions, data, and a careful analysis of that data in scientific investigation.

Communicating Results

FAMILY

CONNECTIONS

Many of us have heard the phrase "publish or perish." For practicing scientists, publishing or presenting their discoveries is often one of the most important aspects of their research. Providing students with authentic methods of communicating their scientific discoveries is equally critical. This communication may take a traditional form, such as an oral presentation or a written report. However, nontraditional methods of communicating discoveries should also be encouraged. Students may decide to make a short film, student website, poster, dramatic recreation, or scientific illustration. You may want to provide opportunities for students to present their results to their family members in their native language, to further cultivate connections between home and school, and between science and students' lives. Providing diverse methods of communicating discoveries will ensure that all students, regardless of their fluency level or preferred learning styles, will be able to showcase and take pride in their developing science knowledge.

Teaching Inquiry-Based Skills in Context

Perhaps the most critical thing to remember is that these steps do not need to be followed in any particular order, nor do all of them need to be used in every learning activity. As we strive to create truly inquiry-based experiences for our students, however, the inclusion of at least one of these processes in every science lesson should be an instructional goal, and the inclusion of more than one process will increase science access for ELLs. It is equally important to remember that science skills should be taught in context. Posing questions that go nowhere, communicating "results" gleaned from reading a textbook—these are not examples of a true inquiry-based approach to instruction. Providing a rich and detailed context, in which students actively participate in science investigation, is a proven approach to supporting content acquisition on the part of all students, and particularly students who are culturally and linguistically diverse (Watson & Houtz, 2002).

Teacher as Facilitator

One of the most critical elements of inquiry is the emphasis on students as leaders in their own learning. Inquiry-based science investigations acknowledge the importance of questions that originate with students' interests and experiences, procedures designed by students, and student-generated results based on original data. So although you are a critical presence who scaffolds all aspects of science learning to create a positive experience for all involved, your role is also one of a facilitator who allows students to take the initiative, whenever possible. In the inquiry process examples just presented, students are active participants in all aspects of the course of learning, from activity design to sharing results. And although a rare few students will be able to breeze through a scientific exploration with little input from you, the majority of students require adequate facilitation and guidance from you to gain the maximum benefit from an inquiry-based science experience.

Effective Use of Questioning

Questioning is a critical part of inquiry-based science. Different from traditional methods of instruction, which focus on teachers posing questions for students to explore and answer, inquiry-based science teaching focuses on student-generated questions. Students experience science best when they are actively engaged in questioning, observing, and exploring. When students explore areas of personal interest, this intrinsically motivated learning results in greater cognitive gains (Covington, 1998). Many students, however, have little experience developing guiding questions. Effective questioning on your part helps support students without moving away from a student-centered learning model. See Example 2.1 for examples of instructor questions that sustain the model of teacher as facilitator.

EXAMPLE 2.1   Sample Questions to Encourage Inquiry

- What are you observing?
- What else would you like to know?
- How could we find that out?
- What materials do you need?
- Is there something you'd like to try?
- Is there another way we could do this?
- What did you find out?
- How do you want to share your discoveries?

Allowing Students to Be the Experts

National standards emphasize the importance of allowing students to take the lead in science explorations (National Research Council, 1996). Research also indicates that teaching content or a skill to others can reinforce our own understanding (Topping et al., 2004). Thus, providing opportunities for students to serve as leaders and experts supports science learning. These types of opportunities might include sharing an experiment or discovery with a peer, a younger grade, or even a parent. Class books, science festivals, or oral presentations are just a few ways for students to share their discoveries. It is important to note, however, that students may harbor misunderstandings about their discoveries. To prevent dissemination of inaccurate information or misconceptions, plan on "consulting" with students during the planning stages to guide them away from inaccuracies, and to help them to discover correct information on their own before they share that information with others.

Integrating Inquiry across the Curriculum

Using an inquiry model is not only appropriate for science. All academic areas can benefit from an inquiry-based approach, and a soundly designed science lesson will naturally integrate other academic subjects in a meaningful way. Many educators are finding that the increased emphasis on language arts and mathematics has diminished the time available for meaningful science lessons. Inquiry-based science experiences will, however, naturally rely heavily on and support language arts and mathematical development, as well as connect with other areas of the curriculum. By integrating subject areas and identifying the ways other areas influence scientific discovery, it is possible to expand opportunities for connecting science, other subjects, and the world beyond the classroom.

Language Arts

Language arts skills are heavily integrated into inquiry-based science in a multitude of ways. Students can develop reading comprehension skills as they gather background information on a selected topic through expository texts, information-rich websites, or field guides (Whitin, 2007). They can build their own expository writing skills as they record data throughout the observation process or while they generate a final report. Oral fluency is developed as students work cooperatively to design investigations and carry them out, making changes as necessary. Communication skills—public speaking and written correspondence—can be developed through e-mail with experts or a final presentation to a group of their peers, family members, or the entire school. Research has indicated that when language arts skills are developed in an authentic context, learning gains can be greater (National Research Council, 1999). Students who may have a learning disability or who are struggling with English fluency often find that their enjoyment of science and hands-on explorations inspires them to take more chances with language and stretch beyond their current performance level. Watching a tortoise walk across the classroom or noting the fizz that is generated when vinegar is mixed with baking soda often prompts even the most reluctant writers to record their exciting observations.

Mathematics

Although not all scientific data that students gather will be quantitative, many inquiry-based activities provide numerous opportunities for the authentic integration of mathematics. Students can develop measurement skills by calculating the height of a growing plant, the circumference of a schoolyard tree, or the weight of different rock samples; or by reading the temperature on a thermometer. To increase cultural relevance, they can compare agricultural production levels, review hurricane patterns, or contrast population demographics between countries. Manipulating any collected data to determine averages, percentages, or totals can support quantification skills as well as provide a real-world context to mathematical computation, which can better support student understanding. Student creation of graphs or charts that reveal and summarize their data is another authentic method of linking science to mathematics. Again, research has indicated that when subjects like science and mathematics are integrated, content comprehension on the part of students is supported (Seki & Menon, 2007).

Fine Arts

A busy classroom day leaves little time for art instruction, although it is often a favorite subject of students. It is also a subject area that can be naturally integrated with inquiry-based science through scientific illustration activities based on students' actual experiences. Scientific illustrations of plants, animals, or scientific processes are found in student textbooks, library selections, and even classroom posters, and can be used as models for illustrations of home-based science (for example, drawing the amount and size of bubbles left after washing dishes in the sink). Older students may focus on detailed illustrations and diagrams that support their understanding of structure and function. Younger students may use the process of scientific illustration to focus their observations. Either way, students develop fine motor skills, color representations, and drawing techniques. Connecting student projects to the work of famous nature illustrators such as Maria Sibylla Merian or John James Audubon provides students with a broader context to the activity (see Sidebar 2.2). They will also be learning a technique that has long been a staple of many practicing scientists.

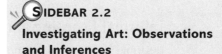

SIDEBAR 2.2

Investigating Art: Observations and Inferences

1. Provide students with works of art from different artists/cultures, such as New Guinea abodes or Amazon rainforests. Better yet, have students select their own works of art to investigate.

2. Ask students to describe what they see (colors, lines). These are *observations*.

3. Now, ask students to infer the mixing of different colors and media versus what the artist is trying to express. These are *inferences*.

4. Discuss how scientists use observations and inferences to gain new knowledge.

Social Studies

Connecting scientific observation to historically significant nature illustrators is just one way to integrate scientific inquiry with topics in social studies. For students to have a true understanding of science as inquiry, it is also important to know the history of scientific thinking and discoveries. While covering topics in social science, try connecting to how science may have played a part in historical events. For example, pairing studies of the Gold Rush with observations of iron pyrite, or "fool's gold," not only authentically links science and social studies, but also provides a physical context and thus increases the relevance of both topics. Think, too, about building on experiences with which students are familiar. For example, most students have experience with cotton balls—the soft, processed balls often stored at home in their bathroom. Combining studies of the difficulties of plantation life can be better explained if students have the option of touching an actual cotton plant with rough edges and sharp points intact, and comparing the end product with the historical processes that brought it here. Identifying the parallels between an inquiry-based approach to science and an inquiry-based approach to social science demonstrates the universal nature of strong research skills (Reap & Rethlefsen, 2006).

Extending the Walls of the Classroom

Informal Learning and Field Trips

Informal learning environments such as museums, zoos, and aquariums are critical components of a well-rounded science curriculum for all students. These experiences can be even more empowering for culturally and linguistically diverse students, who often gain added benefits from the rich context and open-ended nature of these experiences (Melber, 2008; National Science Teachers Association, 1998). Yet, parents who are new to the country may not fully understand the nuances of a field trip and may hesitate to sign a permission slip out of concern that attendance may bring additional costs or may not include adequate adult supervision. For this reason, it is important to explain the details of the trip as well as its purpose through parental correspondence, relying on bilingual translation when possible. Inviting hesitant parents to serve as chaperones during the trip or enlisting the help of a respected room parent are other ways to alleviate fears and to clarify that the field trip is a safe excursion, without additional fees, and is aligned with the classroom learning goals. In addition to these general planning procedures, conducting walking trips with students to areas proximate to the school before any bussed excursions may diminish parental anxieties about subsequent trips afield.

FAMILY

CONNECTIONS

Outdoor Areas and Nature Centers

The opportunity for all students to engage and connect with the natural world is a critical component of a quality science education curriculum. In addition, connection to nature has been shown to support learning and positive behavior for students who may struggle with a learning disability or behavioral difficulties (Louv, 2005). ELLs also benefit from these types of experiences, particularly in their community. Regardless of where a school is situated—be it rural, suburban, or urban—students should be provided with opportunities to investigate their surrounding environment (albeit while keeping safety in mind, such as being cautious along busy streets). Unfortunately, urban students who may benefit most from these experiences have the least opportunity to enjoy them. Moreover, if students do receive the opportunity to engage in nature, it is not uncommon for many to be uncomfortable with expected outcomes. Some families view playing in dirt, touching natural items, or soiling school clothes as things to be avoided. Thus, forewarning and educating parents that getting dirty or touching nature will occur during particular activities, and highlighting safety elements that have been put in place, are necessary preconditions to ensuring outside success (see Sidebar 2.3 for sample correspondence to parents). Regardless of efforts to educate parents, however, some students may need extra encouragement to participate, because of a lack of familiarity with the processes some of us take for granted.

FAMILY CONNECTIONS

Communicating the outcomes of the experience to family members may take a little extra effort as well. Students are notoriously vague when answering the question, "What did you do today?" Accompanied by dirty jeans and a slight sunburn, such vagueness can be confusing and worrisome to parents, especially families who may have been educated in more traditional methods. After a field trip to an outdoor area, send a flyer home that summarizes a few of the activities in which students participated, as well as a couple of questions to prompt further discussion in the home about the experience. Again, when possible, translate materials or, better yet, include pictures of activities with the text.

> ### ⌕ SIDEBAR 2.3
> Sample Letter to Families
>
> *Dear Families,*
> *As you know, we are taking a field trip to the local mountain range next Tuesday. This trip is a good match for our social studies unit on landforms as well as our science unit on plants. Your child will be hiking in natural areas and will most likely get a little dirty as he or she takes part in the assigned activities. We suggest your child wear older play clothes on the day of the trip and sturdy, closed-toe shoes. Because there will be mud and dirt along the trail, older shoes are the best choice.*
>
> *Please feel free to let me know if you have any questions!*
>
> *Mrs. Delamar*

Museums and Science Centers

Although they may cover similar content, the exhibition style and design of natural history museums and science centers can vary widely. Both are excellent places, however, for students to learn about natural history, technology, and concepts in physical science.

The active engagement of science centers is a natural fit for energetic students who are eager to explore content kinesthetically. Teachers need to be aware, however, that it is not uncommon for some students to be so engaged with bells, buttons, and whistles, they do not take the time to explore an exhibit completely and to glean the key information each is designed to deliver. Many children find they are overwhelmed by the newness of a location, such as a science center or museum, and may be unable to focus on content learning. A science center with many working parts and engaging noises may intensify this effect. The best way to overcome this "novelty effect" is to do the following:

- Prepare students in advance about what they will see and do on the trip. Include videos or websites that show actual exhibits.
- Allow students time for free exploration to familiarize themselves with the exhibit areas before bringing them back to an established task or action.

Natural history museums are a common field trip destination, with dinosaurs and life-sized animal dioramas being some of the best-remembered exhibits of many children's early experiences with science. More recent exhibition designs include opportunities for students to engage in active, hands-on scientific investigation, but many still depend on exhibition elements that are more passive or text heavy. Reading label copy may be difficult for ELLs, particularly when the information is located at the base or to the side of an exhibit, absent the context necessary for comprehension. Examine the following list on how to create field trip experiences that are responsive to culturally and linguistically diverse students.

Keys to Culturally Relevant Field Trips

- Provide a brief overview of exhibits in the safety of the classroom during the weeks preceding the trip. Use visuals from museum materials or websites.
- At the museum, focus student attention on the objects rather than the labels. Remind students of key terms and vocabulary discussed earlier in class.
- Ask questions based on prior in-class activities that support and scaffold student comprehension.
- Ask students to compare and contrast what they see, to describe a specimen of great interest, or to create a list of questions they would like to explore further.
- Provide post trip activities that relate to what students saw and did at the museum, and to connect the museum experiences with school and home activities.

Most museums take pride in the extensiveness of their collections, and they house specimens from many parts of the world. You can optimize the museum trip by taking the time to survey what is available for viewing before taking students on the trip:

- Identify those specimens or exhibits that come from students' native (or parents' native) countries.
- Identify specimens that relate to specific standards for your grade level, and students' interests and culture.
- Identify connections between subject areas, cultures, and peoples that can increase students' sense of belonging and relevance. Be sure, however, to support students' recognition of these connections before revealing them.
- Be cautious when discussing differences; not all students want to highlight how their background may be different from that of their peers. Let these students decide whether they wish to identify with the differences being discussed.

Zoos and Aquariums

Children from all backgrounds respond to observations of live animals, but children from different cultures have various views of the role animals play in a society (Bexell et al., 2007). Animals that may be an accepted food source by many in the American culture (such as cattle) are revered as sacred in another. Many animals we see as companion animals or those in need of conservation may be a critical food source in another part of the world. In addition, the idea of an animal in captivity may be looked on as restrictive and harmful by students who may not have a full understanding of the conservation focus of accredited zoos and aquariums in the United States. To mediate these potential concerns, prepare students for the experience in advance to support a positive visit.

When planning excursions to sites with living collections, it is important to create activities that are open-ended and relevant to a variety of students. Younger students may benefit from drawing pictures of the animals they see and writing or dictating simple sentences about animal behavior. Older students may want to compare subtle differences between individuals of the same species or perhaps identify males and females or adults and babies in an exhibition housing multiple animals.

A student investigates sea stars at an aquarium.

Be prepared that students may be fearful of unusual, misunderstood, or unfamiliar animals. During a recent visit to a local aquarium, a fourth-grade teacher couldn't get enough of the smooth and slimy bat rays in the children's touch tank. She was surprised when her students emphatically passed on touching the bat rays and, instead, stood well away from the tank. The best way to support hesitant students is to validate their concerns, always provide an option not to engage, but also offer to share the experience with them (hold their hand, or touch with or before them). Do not be afraid, too, to discuss your own hesitations to particular experiences.

Building Fluency outside the Classroom

Many students who are building their English fluency may be hesitant to practice their English with peers. However, the excitement of animal behavior at the zoo (monkeys caring for babies, or giraffes trying to reach tall branches with their long tongues) can often encourage students to forget their hesitation and chatter away. Review new vocabulary in the classroom before entering the field to help prepare students for what they will encounter. This activity will give them the tools they need to develop their English fluency. Support students' efforts with new vocabulary by asking them to describe what they see to you, a peer, or an adult chaperone. To foster engagement and a sense of belonging, allow the use of students' native languages, particularly during new or unfamiliar experiences.

CASE STUDY   Expect the Unexpected

With limited hours in the day and an unlimited list of things to do, it can be difficult to take advantage of the unplanned yet teachable moments that happen every day. Yet these unplanned learning experiences are often the most effective way to get students engaged in learning. The following is a case study of a fourth-grade teacher named Luis:

I was trying to get the students lined up, but rather than paying attention to me, they were digging into the classroom door jamb. I found myself starting to get annoyed. We had a spelling test to complete and two chapters of social studies to complete before heading home that day.

"But teacher," Yoshi said, "they're all dead!"

Yoshi had arrived from Japan last year and working with him did have its challenges. Because it was difficult to retain his attention under normal circumstances, I was beginning to get curious to see what had him and the other students so enthralled. I looked at what he had dug out of the door jamb and saw he was holding dozens of dead earwigs that the children lovingly called pincer bugs. We had been studying them as part of our habitat unit in science. Yoshi looked at me with a deep frown, "There's so many!"

After a brief moment of contemplation, I broke the children into two groups, half assigned to one classroom door and half to the other. Ten minutes later we had dozens and dozens of dead pincer bugs lined up on a worktable at the back of the classroom. Students immediately began noticing differences in body shapes. It seems we had two species. Among the two species there were more differences. It wasn't long before one student shouted out that the bigger pincers were probably males. After the investigation, students washed their hands and joined me on the rug. Today's task was now focused on solving the mystery of what happened to the pincer bugs. My students who normally were exhausted and sleepy during the last two hours of the day couldn't contain their excitement as they hypothesized how the pincer bugs got into our door jamb.

What started as a mildly annoying interruption to my perfectly planned day turned into a biology lesson well above what I perceived as my fourth-grade students' abilities. At the end of our investigation, we learned that two different species of earwigs lived in our schoolyard, as well as the difference between male and female earwigs, and what a juvenile or baby earwig looks like. Students also practiced their inference skills. For example, as we tried to figure out how our door jambs had filled up with deceased earwigs and nothing else, one of the students remembered that earwigs like to hide in dark places. This explained why they were in the door jambs, but it left us with questions about their demise. Another student who arrived at school early to attend the onsite daycare then mentioned she sometimes saw our custodian spraying the door jambs with something that might be bug spray. The class took all the evidence to propose that the earwigs had walked through the bug spray before crawling into the door jamb to hide.

In one unplanned lesson we addressed animal behavior, environmental science, and insect physiology and development at a level more in line with middle school than fourth grade. It was only possible because I put aside my preset plan to take advantage of a teachable moment. More important, all my students were equally engaged, regardless of literacy level or primary language.

Reflecting on the Case

1. What did this teacher learn about his students and science?
2. How did students extend their learning based on their experiences and observations?
3. How could the teacher enhance this lesson further?

• Book Study Questions •

1. What strategies from this chapter do you see your students enjoying most and therefore motivating them to learn more about science?
2. How can observations help students become more curious?
3. How can you help students develop a different view of scientists rather than the traditional white lab coat and glasses?
4. Why is it important for students to feel confident about themselves as scientists?
5. What is the value of taking students outside the four walls of their classroom to learn science?
6. What field trips could students take in your community to enhance their understanding of science?

References and Suggested Readings

Barman, C. R. (1999). Students' views about scientists and school science: Engaging K–8 teachers in a national study. *Journal of Science Teaching Education, 10*(1), 43–54.

Barnett, M., Lord, C., & Strauss, E. (2006). Using the urban environment to engage youths in urban ecology field studies. *Journal of Environmental Education, 37*(2), 3–11.

Ben-Ari, E. T. (1999). Better than a thousand words: Botanical artists blend science and aesthetics. *BioScience, 49,* 602–608.

Bentley, M. L. (1995). Making the most of the teachable moment: Carpe diem. *Science Activities, 32*(3), 23–27.

Bexell, S. M., Jarrett, O. S., Lan, L., Yan, H., Sandhaus, E. A., Zhibe, Z., & Maple, T. L. (2007). Observing panda play: Implications for zoo programming and conservation efforts. *Curator, 50*(3), 287–298.

Chambers, D. W. (1983). Stereotypic images of the scientist: The Draw-A-Scientist Test. *Science Education, 67,* 253–265.

Covington, M.V. (1998). *The will to learn: A guide for motivating young people.* New York: Cambridge University Press.

Dobb, F. (2004). *Essential elements of effective science instruction for English learners.* 2nd ed. Los Angeles, CA: California Science Project.

Ford, M. J. (2008). Disciplinary authority and accountability in scientific practice and learning. *Science Education, 92*(3), 404–423.

Jongsma, K. (2001). Literacy links between home and school. *Reading Teacher, 55*(1), 58–61.

Kubota, C. A., & Olstad, R. G. (1991). Effects of novelty-reducing preparation on exploratory behavior and cognitive learning in a science museum setting. *Journal of Research in Science Teaching, 28*(3), 225–234.

Laosa, L. M. (1977). Socialization, education, and continuity: The importance of the sociocultural context. *Young Children, 33,* 21–27.

Louv, R. (2005). *Last child in the woods.* Chapel Hill, NC: Algonquin Books.

Mason, C. L., Kahle, J. B., & Gardner, A. L. (1991). Draw-a-Scientist Test: Future implications. *School Science and Mathematics, 91,* 193–198.

McComas, W. F., Clough, M. P., & Almazroa, H. (1998). A review of the role and character of the nature of science in science education. In *The nature of science in science education: Rationales and strategies,* edited by W. F. McComas (pp. 3–39). Dordrecht, Netherlands: Kluwer (Springer) Academic Publishers.

McDonald, R. B. (1997). Using participation in public school "Family Science Night" programs as a component in the preparation of preservice elementary teachers. *Science Education, 81*(5), 577–595.

Melber, L. M. (2008). *Informal learning and field trips.* Thousand Oaks, CA: Corwin Press.

Moreno, R. P. (1991). Maternal teaching of preschool children in minority and low-status families: A critical review. *Early Childhood Research Quarterly, 6,* 395–410.

National Council for the Social Studies. (1994). *Expectations of excellence: Curriculum standards for social studies.* Silver Springs, MD: National Council for the Social Studies.

National Research Council. (1996). *National science education standards.* Washington, DC: National Academy Press.

National Research Council. (1999). *How people learn: Brain, mind, experience, and school.* Washington, DC: National Academy Press.

National Science Teachers Association. (1998). NSTA position statement on informal science education. *Journal of College Science Teaching, 28,* 17–18.

Reap, M. A., & Rethlefsen, A. L. (2006). Examining the westward movement through a new lens: The Donner party. *Social Studies, 97*(2), 51–55.

Seki, J. M., & Menon, R. (2007). Incorporating mathematics into the science program of students labeled "at risk." *School Science and Mathematics, 107*(2), 61–69.

Topping, K. J., Peter, C., Stephen, P. & Whale, M. (2004). Cross-age peer tutoring of science in the primary school: Influence on scientific language and thinking. *Educational Psychology, 24*(1), 57–75.

Tunnicliffe, S. D., & Reiss, M. H. (2000). What sense do children make of three-dimensional, life-sized "representations" of animals? *School Science and Mathematics, 100*(3), 128–137.

van Eijck, M., & Roth, W.- M. (2008). Representations of scientists in Canadian high school and college textbooks. *Journal of Research in Science Teaching, 45*(9), 1059–1082.

Watson, S. M. R., & Houtz, L. E. (2002). Teaching science: Meeting the academic needs of culturally and linguistically diverse students. *Intervention in School and Clinic, 37,* 267–278.

Whitin, P. (2007). The ties that bind: Emergent literacy and scientific inquiry. *Language Arts, 85*(1), 20–30.Dici aliam simustis rectur sit ea suntur? Quis simaiore pelectur saeceatur ant.

Literacy Development through Science

• Prior Knowledge and Beliefs Organizer •

- Describe how literacy can help with understanding science content.
- Describe how literacy can help with understanding science and what scientists do.

Consider your responses to the questions posed above as you read about how to enhance literacy development through science concepts and activities in this chapter.

Importance of Authentic Connections

It has been established that context is critical to building language arts skills for most students. This is particularly important for linguistically and culturally diverse students. *Language arts* skills include reading, writing, listening, and speaking. *Literacy* includes reading and writing. In this chapter we use the word *literacy* to include all the language arts when teaching and learning science. Research has indicated that experiences with inquiry-based science methods are critical to literacy development and to providing students with authentic opportunities to develop in both science and literacy (see, for example, Amarah et al. [2002]). Many ELLs may find that stretching their literacy skills in the context of inquiry-based science can be enjoyable, and it may encourage them to be more motivated in learning and understanding scientific phenomena (Westervelt, 2007).

The key to creating truly authentic science experiences is to focus on the use of literacy skills practiced by scientists. This is comprised of looking beyond simply including science vocabulary on a spelling list, or ensuring there is a science book or two in a classroom library. True integration of science and literacy involves systematic inclusion of language arts activities at every stage of scientific investigation to parallel actual scientific research. These real-world applications of language arts are an important part of a successful language arts program for all students (Gutherie et al., 2000) and will specifically support ELLs by adding

- Relevancy
- Context
- Motivating content

Language Arts and the Work of Scientists

Communication skills are critical to practicing scientists at all stages, including the research and reporting process. As mentioned in Chapter 2, it is important for scientists to share their work with their peers and the general public by presenting their work at conferences or by publishing articles. Literacy plays a part during all stages of the research process, from recording data and reading research studies to sending e-mail to colleagues halfway around the world. By creating experiences like these for students, you'll provide authentic inquiry-based experiences and a forum for literacy development. Observation journals and data notebooks are tools that can help promote literacy while students engage in authentic science activities.

Science Notebooks and Journals

It's rare to see a scientist working without something on which to take notes. Scientific inquiry involves a lot of observations. Recording these data is critical for use in later analysis as well as to guide a researcher toward a new field of study. Encouraging students to keep science journals or notebooks is one way to support literacy development along with building inquiry skills.

There is a multitude of ways to use science notebooks or journals, with specific approaches that are best for one grade level over another. Even the terms *notebook* and *journal* are used in different ways by different educators. In this section, we'll explore two models of journal/notebook use that strengthen different elements of the inquiry process and support students with their development of writing skills.

Observation Journals

As noted, observations are a critical part of the inquiry process. Many scientists use general, unstructured observations to lead them to a field for more rigorous and methodical study. An observation journal can be a place in which students can

- Tally what they see outside a schoolyard window
- Describe the growth and flowering of an indoor plant
- Record patterns of clouds in the sky

Observation journals provide opportunities for students to explore areas of interest, to carry out observation skills, and to practice recording data with less structure than a preset observation sheet. When you allow students to draw what they observe, in addition to writing, this open-ended structure is especially helpful for ELLs at varying levels of literacy development. Down the line, you may have students refer to their observation journals when they need to select a question they may want to explore further, or review how their abilities to describe what they see develops throughout the year. Because the emphasis is on observation, it is important to provide students with firsthand experiences. This may include allowing them access to the schoolyard during journal time, or bringing items like fruit, flowers, melting ice, or rocks into the classroom for them to describe.

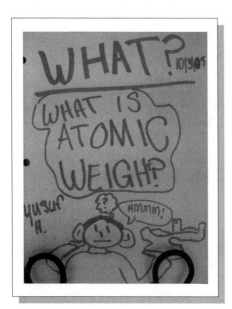

Student questions lead to inquiry.

Many educators already have daily journal writing as a part of the classroom routine. You may choose to make these journals only science focused, especially if there is little other time during the day to incorporate science. Another option is to select several days each week when topics must be science related. Assessing observation journals can take many forms, depending on both age and literacy level of students. Chapter 5 provides more information on assessment strategies to support culturally and linguistically diverse students. Sharing selected entries orally can be also incorporated to provide oral language development opportunities.

Data Notebooks

Recording data is at the center of scientific inquiry. By recording data rather than relying on memory, it's more likely that the data are accurate when researchers reach the analysis portion of a study. Sometimes looking over a data set recorded over time can bring to light new questions for research or may highlight findings very different from what was expected. Some students may think data are only numbers, such as counts or measurements. By asking your students to maintain a data notebook, you are showing them that qualitative descriptions are also data and have a critical place in inquiry-based studies.

As students participate in scientific explorations, remind them to do the following:

- Compile all data into a notebook to reinforce the reality of a large volume of data.
- Develop a continuous recording of data in the form of tables or charts to organize data.
- Include dates, time, descriptions, and other important information.
- Continue to collect data during different scientific investigations throughout the school year.

Different types of data sheets or notebook guidelines develop different types of writing skills. Data notebooks may be bound, lined paper; however, using open-ended data sheets supports students who are still building English fluency, and again, particularly when they are allowed to draw as well as write their ideas.

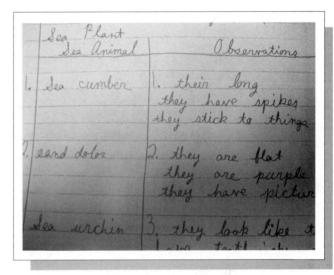

A student's sample observation journal.

Reviewing Information Sources

A scientist who doesn't read background information or studies by other researchers wouldn't be a very good scientist. Reviewing existing information on the Internet, in books, or from journals before beginning a study is a critical step in the inquiry process. Being able to analyze this information critically to determine its accuracy and relevancy to the question at hand is an additional skill that must be mastered. Access to a variety of reading material is a critical component of a balanced literacy program (Frey et al., 2005); use of printed material supports both inquiry-based science and a balanced language arts program. This section explores how to incorporate informational texts and other printed material aligned in the inquiry process. In addition, analyzing reading material critically promotes awareness in students.

Science Textbooks

The use of textbooks as part of the science curriculum has a long history. However, this section explores moving past reading a textbook chapter and answering essay questions at the end. When was the last time a scientific researcher did that? Using the textbook as an information source and guide is a better option, rather than relying on it as the sole source of information. Very little inquiry can be promoted with simply reading a science text. Nevertheless, science textbooks are visually stimulating.

Some research indicates that textbooks in a number of content areas are often written at a level above what many ELLs are prepared to read (see Brown [2007], for example). As a remedy to these and other issues, consider using the textbook as you would any other resource book that students turn to for information as part of an investigation. Some teachers find textbooks

- Provide students with background content on a new subject more quickly and efficiently
- Help pace or determine the order in which units are delivered
- Encourage students to analyze the information in their science text critically, which promotes more significant inquiry into the types of information available and the power associated with different types of science content
- Feature brightly colored diagrams and dynamic images such as volcanoes erupting or lions chasing prey

Informational Texts

Informational texts are nonfiction books that focus on single or multiple science topics. They provide an excellent opportunity for students to exercise reading comprehension skills and to read for specific information. Selecting informational texts with vivid images will be especially important and motivating for ELLs. Images that portray specific concepts will assist ELLs, who may still be developing English fluency, with reading comprehension and vocabulary. Although the most current books are the most helpful in providing up-to-date content information, outdated books can be equally useful in the classroom. A critical thinking exercise based on reading comprehension can include having students review exceptionally outdated books after the close of a unit to highlight information that is no longer accurate based on their new content knowledge and discoveries.

Newspapers and Journals

Journal articles are the preferred source of scientific information for most scientists. Books can quickly become outdated whereas journals are published weekly or monthly. In addition, most journal articles have been reviewed and accepted by other scientists. Books go through a different review process that may not check the science as carefully, depending on the type of publication. Encourage students to explore other forms of written information. Although journal articles used by researchers are likely too difficult for younger students to comprehend, children's magazines that focus on science and the environment are a good substitute. Clearly, newspapers have many articles and images that are not appropriate for students. However, by pulling out science articles and sections for students, they can be resources for current science stories as well as a barometer for public interest in different types of science stories. They can also highlight the global nature of scientific investigation. Newspaper articles in languages other than English are a nice addition to a project. Encourage students to share science articles from community and local newspapers as well as newspapers written in their native language.

Sharing Discoveries

Communicating discoveries is a critical part of inquiry-based science. Connecting school, home, and community is an important part of an effective and well-balanced curriculum for literacy and scientific development as well. Disseminating information, communicating with scientists, and viewing science as a global community are ways that students can share data and engage in more authentic investigations. These activities are discussed in this section.

Disseminating Information to Peers, Families, and the Community

FAMILY

CONNECTIONS

Scientists use a variety of dissemination methods, including presenting at professional conferences, writing journal articles and books, as well as creating museum exhibitions. To mirror this process, you can encourage your students to use a range of methods to communicate their discoveries. Sharing with peers, family members, and the broader community is critical to the scientific and literacy development process. Encourage students to think creatively about how best to communicate what they learned with their classmates, younger students, older peers, families, and community members. Your students may opt to do one of the following activities to promote oral and written literacy, and to report their scientific findings:

- Create PowerPoint slides and present their findings to the class or a larger group
- Construct an abstract, in the form of a single paragraph, that highlights their major findings of their investigation; this can be published in a school or community newspaper
- Create a display board with a few key sentences, and images and diagrams to illustrate their findings
- Write a children's book that highlights important facts about scientific content, and share the book with families and younger students in the school
- Create a museum exhibition to share their discoveries
- Write a book to leave in the school library, hang a poster in the cafeteria, or do an oral presentation for another grade level

- Create postcards, letters, posters, science exploration evenings, or newsletters
- Develop a webpage to share what they have learned, which is another way that students can stretch their literacy skills

Communicating with Scientists

Students are often encouraged to communicate with a scientist as part of the information-gathering phase of a project. It is important that students connect with scientists, but also have your students contact other science experts as well. By expanding your definition of scientist to include subject matter experts, graduate students, or undergraduate science majors, you create the opportunity to tap into a variety of expertise. A parent who successfully grows orchids, or a neighbor who is a veterinarian can provide critical information on how plants grow or how long a hamster might live, respectively.

Before having students contact experts or friends, first find out the preferred method of contact and their willingness to participate. This helps to expedite a response. To develop student literacy skills further, encourage your students to write e-mail messages and letters that contain a specific question. Letters that start, "Tell me everything you know about dinosaurs," will most likely go unanswered. Correspondence that asks, "Can you tell me how long a Basset Hound may live?" is more specific and is easier to tackle in a short response.

Viewing Science as a Global Community

Scientists from all over the world work together in their efforts to understand their environment. It is not unusual for a scientist to travel halfway around the globe to collect data or to co-author a paper with a colleague in a different country. Highlight scientists and science stories from around the world to bring different cultures into the classroom in an authentic way and to call attention to diversity among practicing scientists, which is especially important when working with ELLs. Students of color are currently underrepresented in many scientific fields (National Science Foundation, 2006). Give these students authentic images of the diversity that exists to support them in viewing science as a viable career choice to explore.

Encourage students to share their work beyond the classroom and local community when possible. Provide opportunities for students to communicate their discoveries to students in other parts of the state, country, or world. Students from different places can collect data and share this information. Here are some ways to do this:

- Contact a school in a different city or state via e-mail. Have students create a letter stating who they are, what data they are interested in sharing, and directions on how the school/class can participate.
- Determine how many different schools you would like to share data with and the type of environment where the school is located. For example, if you want to collect information about pigeon behavior and types, then you might contact schools in urban environments.

If you want to collect diverse environmental data related to different types of birds, you might contact schools in a variety of areas such as rural, suburban, and urban. Sharing information with students in schools around the world is very exciting.

- After the data have been collected by students from different schools, determine how the data will be shared: website, e-mail, virtual science conference, or some other way.

Extending the Experience

Selecting science as a career is not the only way people experience science in their lives. In addition to providing language arts activities that align with the work of scientists, highlight integration opportunities that support student appreciation and enjoyment of science and the natural world. From poetry to picture books, there are a number of other ways to integrate language arts activities to support science learning by tapping into the natural creativity of your students.

Children inquire informally about the life cycle of a butterfly in a comfortable environment within the classroom.

Fictional Texts

A former colleague of ours was fond of the phrase "never let the truth get in the way of a good story." Although this goes against the very nature of science, Mrs. Brown does raise a critical point. Students love to be drawn in by fantasy and fanciful stories. A caterpillar that eats cupcakes or a child who travels through time captures students' imagination and piques their interest in the written word. Although some may argue such texts have no place in a science curriculum, many others disagree. Consider building on student interest in fictional texts—chapter books or picture books—and draw them into your science unit as opportunities for critical analysis. Younger students can explore a picture book as a class and highlight which parts are accurate and which parts are "creative" (as a fictional book, use of the word *wrong* is a bit harsh). ELLs may especially benefit from this group analysis, which will help support reading comprehension. Older students can conduct individual analyses of chapter books, such as deconstructing a science fiction book and tying it to current events in physical and space science.

This is also an opportunity to include folktales and myths from different cultures that are related to natural phenomena. As you explore true causes, however, be cautious not to discredit or marginalize how these cultural traditions may explain scientific happenings; instead, maintain respectful treatment of these traditions.

Including poetry as part of a science unit can tap into students' emotions and potential affective gains of a quality science curriculum. The shorter length of poems coupled with personal word selection may be considered more manageable by students who are still building English fluency.

Dramatic Play

Many students love to participate in dramatic play. Sometimes this creative outlet is a more engaging place for ELLs to develop fluency skills and is an opportunity for reciprocal sharing for students from diverse cultures. Content from science units can be incorporated easily into a student performance format. You might have students' role-play a scientist at work, reenact an environmental debate, or take on the character of natural phenomena such as rain or lightning to explain their origin. Add a catchy song to help students remember key themes from lessons; this is a helpful and enjoyable addition to a performance.

CASE STUDY A Community Service Project to Encourage
Shared Decision Making

Sixth-grade teacher Bridget Burke works with her students to engage in a community service project that encourages shared decision making among students, and integrates literacy and other subjects with science and social studies. The following is a letter that she sent to parents of students in her class based on student-initiated topics.

Dear Parents,
During the next two quarters, your students will become "Active Citizens" in our community.

Our science and social studies class has worked extremely hard to research issues, causes, and organizations where we can focus on a integrated learning project. Please ask your child to discuss the following choices and, as a family, select one of the following causes:

☐ *CHOC Hospital*   ☐ *Wyss Family*
☐ *Carol & Stacey*   ☐ *Lymphoma/Leukemia*
☐ *Breast Cancer*   ☐ *Sponsor Two Malawi Children in Africa*
☐ *San Clemente Animal Shelter* ☐ *American Cancer Society*
☐ *Surfrider Foundation*   ☐ *Homeless Shelter*
☐ *Recycle Containers for BAMS*

Please deliberate over the weekend. Your final choice is due Monday, with signatures!

_____   _____
Student Signature   *Parent Signature*

Our goal is to host a fund-raiser in the form of a silent/live auction, including a bake sale. The proceeds from the fund-raiser will go directly to benefit one family, organization, or community issue with the most votes from the causes listed above.

After the votes are counted, we will focus our efforts on only one cause/issue. Students will learn how to develop an action plan and form class committees to do tasks such as the following:

- Research resources and create PowerPoint slides
- Present solutions to the problem
- Deliberate alternatives
- Write letters to recruit partnerships in our community
- Design pamphlets and posters
- Write public service announcements
- Evaluate and reflect on positive differences
- Discover the process of fund-raising
- Reinforce our class "life skills"

*PERSEVERANCE * PROBLEM SOLVING * COMMON SENSE * FRIENDSHIP *

* SENSE OF HUMOR * INTEGRITY * FLEXIBILITY *

* ORGANIZATION * COURAGE * INITIATIVE *

* COOPERATION * EFFORT * PATIENCE *

* CARING * CURIOSITY *

* RESPONSIBILITY *

And **passionately experience that we all can make a powerful difference!**

Reflecting on the Case

1. How did Mrs. Burke incorporate shared decision-making strategies in this service learning assignment?
2. What literacy and math skills could be enhanced through this project?
3. What science content and skills could be learned through this project?

• Book Study Questions •

1. What are some ways that you can incorporate literacy into science?
2. Describe how you might use your science text more creatively.
3. Indicate how you would help students to challenge different sources of science knowledge such as online materials, textbooks, and science trade books.

4. Make a list of potential companies, universities, or other organizations that employ scientists. With which scientists could students communicate to enhance their understanding of science?

5. How could you assist students when learning to read for information in a variety of materials?

6. How could science notebooks be integrated into your science lessons?

• References and Suggested Readings •

Amarah, O. M., Garrison, L., & Klentschy, M. (2002). Helping English learners increase achievement through inquiry based science instruction. *Bilingual Research Journal, 26,* 213–239.

Brown, C. L. (2007). Strategies for making social studies texts comprehensible for English language learners. *The Social Studies, 98,* 185–188.

Colon-Vila, L. (1997). Story telling in an ESL classroom. *Teaching Pre K–8, 27,* 58–59.

Frey, B. B., Lee, S. W., Tollfson, N., Pass, L., & Massengill, D. (2005). Balanced literacy in an urban school district. *Journal of Educational Research, 98,* 272–280.

Gutherie, J. T., Wigfield, A., & Vonsecker, C. (2000). Effects of integrated instruction on motivation and strategy use in reading. *Journal of Educational Psychology, 92,* 331–341.

Medina-Jerez, W., Clark, D. B., Medina, A., & Ramirez-Marin, F. (2007). Science for ELLs: Rethinking our approach. *The Science Teacher, 74,* 52–56.

National Research Council. (1999). *How people learn: Brain, mind, experience, and school.* Washington, DC: National Academy Press.

National Science Foundation. (2010). *Science and engineering indicators 2010.* Retrieved March 11, 2011, from www.nsf.gov/statistics/seind10/.

National Science Teachers Association. (2002). NSTA position statement: Elementary school science. Retrieved March 1, 2009, from www.nsta.org/about/positions/elementary.aspx.

Westervelt, M. (2007). Schoolyard inquiry for English language learners. *The Science Teacher, 74,* 47–51.

Models and Strategies for Teaching Science Content and Skills

• Prior Knowledge and Beliefs Organizer •

- Jot down the types of teaching strategies that you use when teaching science to encourage success for all students.

- Which strategies best help students connect school science with science in their neighborhoods, homes, and communities?

In this chapter we present traditional teaching models in a way that encourages more culturally relevant teaching and learning. Before we discuss the different models, we review characteristics of learning, and how children become interested in knowledge and how they become motivated to learn.

Learner Differences

We generally prefer one style of teaching to another, and we tend to teach in the ways with which we are the most comfortable. Yet, when we think about it, we know there is no single "best" mode for teaching; there is no one-size-fits-all instructional approach that works for everyone. We all learn differently, and thus we need to ensure that we pull from as many instructional modes as possible when designing science instruction. Culturally relevant instruction recognizes this (indeed, it depends on it!) and advocates integrating multiple strategies to promote a comfortable and motivating environment for all students, regardless of their learning style, native language, culture, or academic achievement.

One easy way to integrate diverse teaching strategies is to think of the act of teaching like it is a Japanese *bento* box: a whole that is filled with distinct parts, each of which works to meet a nutritional—or in the case of teaching, educational—need. Fill your *bento* box with instruction that is visual, auditory, and kinesthetic. Ensure that each lesson tries to hit all three (or at least two) of these dimensions, so that you tap into students' preferred learning styles, while regularly exposing them to other styles. The use of multiple instructional modes reflects the nature of science itself—a field in which scientists regularly depend and build on multiple processes in the search for solutions. By representing science practice more accurately through a variety of processes that build on students' preferred learning styles, you can make science more meaningful and interesting.

Motivating Students by Building on Their Interests in Science

There is an array of literature and research findings related to motivation and its effect on learning, and there are many factors involved in motivating students. Provoking or developing interest in a particular subject is one such motivator. If students like science, then they will want to learn more about it. Thus, it is important to take the time to find out *what interests students*. Here we are talking about what is relevant to students' cultures (in other words, each individual's developing, dynamic, and changing interests and culture) in your development of science lessons and activities.

We remember a fifth grader, Rick, who was essentially a nonreader. He knew various sight words and could sound out some words, but he often had difficulty comprehending what he was reading. When we introduced an open-ended project where he could inquire into a marine animal of his choice, however, this motivated him to want to read. He conducted extensive research using a variety of sources about moray eels and leopard sharks, and then created a PowerPoint presentation for his classmates.

Another factor that motivates students in learning relates to their perception of a subject or skill's usefulness in their lives. You can serve as a conduit to help students connect science at school with learning at home or with a particular purpose by ensuring students' instruction is meaningful and resonates with them in real, practical ways. If students are participating in a service learning project in which they are investigating pollution in their communities or neighborhoods (and if they are able to choose what they want to investigate), then they will more likely take a vested interest in the activity.

The Role of Self-Confidence and Self-Efficacy

Self-confidence and self-efficacy play major roles in motivating students to learn about science. Both of these traits are particularly valuable in science, because students' self-efficacy (the belief in oneself or one's ability to perform or demonstrate knowledge) can affect their achievement in school. When science is presented in culturally *ir*relevant ways, however, students who are not part of the dominant culture often have far less confidence approaching science than their white, middle-class counterparts, and science itself becomes more difficult. Thus, bolstering all students' capacity in science is key to increasing achievement in science. Connections made between students, their environments, and their behavior (motivation) influence how they value learning, whether they take initiative in their learning, and whether they continue to want to learn.

The levels of self-confidence and self-efficacy students feel can be enhanced through culturally relevant content and activities. Identifying issues affecting human, animal, or plant populations in students' native countries, and investigating the causes of population changes can interest students in ways that traditional science textbook lessons cannot. Tracking the agricultural science involved in producing crops for export from one country to another can be similarly engaging. Examining environmental science in an urban community can open students' eyes to the science all around them. Mentors involved in science projects or studies at local universities or high schools can be helpful when they are from similar ethnic, linguistic, or cultural backgrounds as younger elementary students. These mentors can be science buddies through the length of a unit or throughout an entire school year (or longer), and can work with students on science projects during school or after school, and can communicate via e-mail. Cultivating relationships with older students establishes a mentoring process early and provides a sense of connection, contact, and security that can enhance younger students' motivation for learning science.

Here we outline a few specific strategies derived from the previous discussion that can aid in motivating students in science. Three overarching focal points are identified: interest in science, usefulness of science in students' everyday lives, and self-confidence/self-efficacy.

Interest in science can be enhanced by

- Using vocabulary and visual or hands-on examples that relate to students' interest and everyday lives; connecting new vocabulary to students' experiences
- Engaging students in the totality of the learning process by allowing them to determine instructional topics or directions based on adopted academic standards
- Connecting science to issues important in students' native countries, their communities, or their families; encouraging active involvement of science by the whole family by inviting family members to participate in class science activities
- Extending science outside the classroom, including museums, zoos, and local parks

FAMILY

CONNECTIONS

Usefulness of science in students' everyday lives can be enhanced by

- Discussing relevance of the science content and activities in relation to individual student lives, family experiences, or community concerns

- Doing science as often as reading about it; creating activities that depend on experiments, interaction, and inquiry to make science more meaningful and relevant to students' daily lives

- Assigning science homework that considers and examines the area around the school and students' homes

Self-confidence and self-efficacy in science can be enhanced by

- Sharing authority with students so they learn to make decisions with you and their peers

- Providing opportunities for students to interact with their peers before science activities so they can predict what will occur, to collaborate during science activities, and to debrief others after science activities

FAMILY

CONNECTIONS

- Providing opportunities for students to interact with mentors or other community members who represent their ethnic, cultural, or socioeconomic group

- Maintaining high expectations for all students, and encouraging students to reflect on their own learning and development regularly

The Value of Creative Thinking

Creative thinking can be integrated and developed in science instruction to empower students less familiar or comfortable with the traditional linear science curriculum. Puccio and Murdock (2001) claim that creative thinking involves the generation of new ideas, but it also includes the various ways that ideas are constructed and communicated. Providing students with opportunities to think outside the box (and the traditional textbook), as well as supporting a variety of methods of sharing and communicating what they learn, can foster authentic interest in science.

What is great about creative thinking in relation to science is that it can be built around inductive or deductive thought processes. With *inductive processes,* students collect a variety of information from different sources and then generate ideas based on their collected information. With *deductive processes,* students take a larger topic or idea, such as "all living organisms are made of structures and have specific functions," collect information on this larger idea, and then conduct investigations related to it. Through meaningful experiences with both of these processes, students learn to distinguish between the two processes and determine which to apply when faced with new science challenges. At every stage in creative thinking, students develop their capacity to identify what matters; to collect and organize relevant information, materials, and data; and to generate conclusions based on choices they have made and what their collected data support.

Providing a variety of materials for students to manipulate and investigate also enhances creative thinking. These materials can be specifically science related, such as microscopes, hand lenses, and other equipment, or they can be materials for general use, such as measuring cups, balance scales, and everyday objects found around the house or the classroom. Real, tangible materials inspire curiosity and provoke questions. Ensuring students have regular exposure to tangible items in science facilitates an understanding of science as something real and meaningful that can be discussed with others.

Some students are more creative when given opportunities to work independently, whereas other students are more creative when working in social situations. You can provide opportunities for students to be creative in a variety of situations by instituting flexible grouping in science lessons. Whether they work in small groups or alone, however, it is important to allow all students to share their ideas and to ask for feedback from their peers. It is particularly important for ELLs to have many opportunities to share with their more English-proficient peers. ELLs should be provided with multiple opportunities for discussion with peers to develop their English proficiency (through more casual, less academically risky conversation and more content-focused discussions) and to cultivate relationships with more English-proficient students in the class.

Two girls work together to build parts of a house.

Encouraging Critical Thinking and Metacognition

Critical thinking is related to creative thinking, but it involves more specific mental constructs and processes for the purposes of solving problems or making decisions. Thus, it involves activities like evaluating, reflecting, classifying, hypothesizing, analyzing, and reasoning (Fisher, 2001). Fisher (2001) posits that teachers can scaffold critical thinking by posing a variety of meaningful and provocative questions that may puzzle students or cause conflict in their thinking and may engender curiosity or interest. For example, you could fill a large container with water and place several different fruits from around the world in the water, such as a lime, coconut, papaya, mango, rambutan, and lychee. Students will notice that some of the fruit sinks and some floats. Ask students to discuss what they see and to provide some rationale to describe the differences they see. During these types of culturally relevant science activities, you can support content comprehension (by focusing on why some fruit floats and other fruit does not), increasing interest in science (by determining what makes the difference in the fruit that floats), and English language development (by encouraging students to talk with one another about what they see). Focusing more on *how* or *why*

To develop critical thinking exercises in the classroom, begin by working with students to distinguish between different types of science activities and experiments. Encourage them to describe the characteristics of science activities, ask them about the process of doing things in science, and ask them how what they are learning relates to things they have experienced. A simple, key question that aids in increasing students' understanding of the metacognitive aspects of learning is: How did you get this answer? When you ask students to describe their thinking process, you draw their attention to it and consequently show them that you value *their* thinking— a win–win situation! In addition, when students describe their thinking processes, they can distinguish between the type of activity and the degree to which you defined the problem, activity, and results, as well as to what extent students were involved in the process. The following table can help you identify how your instructional activities are focused and directed (to or for students or teachers), and whether you are diversifying focus and direction within science units of study.

questions, rather than *what* questions, encourages more active and critical thinking, and generates enthusiasm for science and solving science problems. A critical analysis of text materials and other resources also provides a way for students to reflect on different types of information and to draw conclusions based on a variety of evidence.

Metacognition is part of critical thinking. It involves thinking about the process of thinking, or reflecting. In classrooms, a focus on metacognition involves helping students ponder their own thoughts and views, as well as the thoughts of others. Hartman (1998) explains that metacognition affects the acquisition, comprehension, and retention of content learned, which in turn affects learning efficacy, critical thinking, and problem solving. During science experiments and activities, students can ask specific questions to reflect on their thinking and learning, such as "What do I know about this topic?" or "What strategies worked best?" and "What can I improve so that I work more efficiently or better next time?"

Distinguishing between Teacher- and Student-Driven Activities

	Defining the Problem or Asking a Question	Defining the Procedure or Task to Answer the Question or to Solve the Problem	Determining Results
Teacher-directed	Teacher	Teacher	Teacher
Teacher-focused	Teacher	Teacher	Teacher and students
Student-directed	Teacher	Students	Students
Student-focused	Students	Students	Students

Integrating Cognitive Views of Learning

A *social cognitive view of learning* contends that students learn in social environments and social situations (Schunk, 2008). In this view, students' knowledge is a result of understanding the rules, strategies, beliefs, and attitudes to which they are exposed in science instruction (for example, through observation and the modeling of others around them). Learning, therefore, occurs through interactive experiences and *doing,* as well as by *observing.* Like social cognitive theory, *constructivist theories* also emphasize the role of students' active engagement in instruction (learning by doing), their experiences, and their prior knowledge. Based on the work of Vygotsky (1978), constructivists argue that knowledge is constructed within the context of social and language processes with the teacher, other students, and the community. In general, Vygotsky's social constructivism posits that knowledge is socially created with others; the learner is at the center of knowing when interacting with adults and peers. In constructivism, teachers take roles as facilitators of knowledge construction, rather than as transmitters of information. Vygotsky's *zone of proximal development* (Vygotsky, 1978) is the gray area between what students can do on their own and how they become more competent working with a teacher or other person who scaffolds their understanding with questions, interaction, and guidance. You have an important role in constructivism; you scaffold student comprehension of science concepts over time and through active engagement with scientific inquiry, because your students may not necessarily be able to create a scientifically accurate understanding alone. As your students become more knowledgeable, your role is reduced.

These cognitive views of learning provide the basis for many instructional strategies related to attaining concepts, including concept maps and two teaching models: concept formation and concept attainment. These strategies and models are presented in the next section and focus on optimizing cultural relevance. The elaborations that follow are derived from the culturally relevant strategies discussed in Chapter 1 and in this chapter—namely,

- Redistributing authority and redefining classroom responsibilities
- Cultivating and nurturing positive scientific attitudes by connecting science to students' home lives
- Scaffolding content and supporting student awareness of metacognitive processes in learning
- Developing students' capacity to think independently, critically, and creatively
- Encouraging real, active, and engaged conversations
- Extending and connecting content and relationships beyond the classroom

Notice in the following pages that we have diversified focal points in each section; some of the models focus more on connecting to students' home lives whereas others focus more on supporting metacognitive processes and cultivating positive scientific attitudes. All models, however, discuss scaffolding content, generating genuine and meaningful dialogue, and redistributing authority as integral parts of instruction.

Concept Maps

Understanding science involves understanding broad science concepts. A *concept* is a labeled set of objects or ideas that share common characteristics (Schunk, 2008). *Concept maps* can help students understand and attain concepts. They will also help you to assess students' prior knowledge, understanding of science concepts, and organization of specific ideas. Usually, concept maps include a general term or concept in the center of a sheet of paper, and various offshoots and ideas that relate to the concept are placed around the general term or concept. Students generate ideas and show characteristics or relationships between science concepts by drawing lines from the center of the page to other areas. Concept maps can be an effective teaching and assessment tool, *but* you must be explicit and

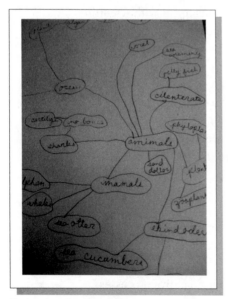

- Teach students *how* to create concept maps
- Guide students while talking through creating concept maps, and highlight key relationships and connections while developing the maps
- Show students examples of different types of concept maps
- Provide lots of time for students to practice concept mapping

Before creating their own maps and after you have given them ample opportunities for practice and feedback on their ideas, students can work in small groups to create concept maps based on collaborative ideas. Concepts maps are viewed as a culturally relevant tool because students determine what goes where. Based on their understanding of science, they can record their ideas in their native language (if appropriate), and can show how they organize their own understanding of science concepts and terms. You can scaffold students' understanding of science by discussing, questioning, and clarifying students' placement of particular items in their concept maps. Students and teachers alike share understandings of *why* certain things have ended up in certain places on the concept map.

Example of a concept map.

Concept Formation Model of Instruction

Concept formation is a model of teaching that can help students build richer and deeper ideas related to science concepts. The model requires that students classify and organize ideas or objects based on relationships they see and can support. This is an inductive teaching model because students brainstorm a variety of ideas and then categorize the ideas into larger concepts. While focusing on a specific science concept, students suggest a series of ideas related to the concept, group their ideas, and then name them. Using concept formation depends on students sharing and building on their prior ideas and understanding, before they organize their ideas into larger, overarching categories or themes. When used appropriately, this is a culturally relevant approach, because the "information" or instructional material comes from students as they think of ideas, determine groups, and label these groups based on their own ideas, experiences, and any resources provided. You can begin to use concept formation in science by asking about science in the home.

Specific steps related to concept formation are provided in Table 4.1, along with a sample lesson. The first question in the table—What sort of science happens in your home?—is purposefully general and open-ended, because you want to find out what your students think science *is*. Thus, you ask them. Then you use concept formation to see not only what they think science *is* (the "listing" part), but also how they think sorts of science relate (the "grouping" part).

TABLE 4.1   Concept Formation Model

1. Begin with a *question* or *concept* related to science standards *and* connected to students' lives. For example: What sort of science happens in your home?	*Redistributing authority:* Ask students to generate some topics related to the science standards under study. Students determine concepts based on science standards and their individual experiences in school and at home.
2. *Brainstorm* a list of ideas related to the concept or question. Be sure to ask extending questions, so students learn that you value what they have to say and that you want to understand what science is from their perspective.	*Encouraging real conversations:* Prompt students to share their own thoughts and experiences when they list their ideas. When you ask about science at home, this shows your interest in their home life. Consider keeping a box of vocabulary cards and picture cards to supplement the verbal list generated by brainstorming. Cards with pictures will help to ensure the involvement and comprehension of ELLs. When possible, pull a picture card to add to the corresponding terms written on the student-generated list.

(Continued)

TABLE 4.1 Concept Formation Model (*Continued*)

3. *Group ideas* according to attributes or similarities.	*Redistributing authority/scaffolding:* Instruct students to complete the grouping task. Facilitate the process, scaffolding when appropriate, and ask students to apply their reasoning and critical thinking skills to the process. Ask questions such as: Which of these things belong together? Why would you group them this way? What is another way you could group them?
4. *Label* the groups derived from Step 3.	*Scaffolding and critical analysis:* Tell students to determine the grouping labels based on their experiences and any resources available. Facilitate the discussion. *Examining authority/critical analysis/discourse:* Encourage students to distinguish between different resources and information when determining the labels for their groups. They must explain their reasoning behind their groups and their labels.
5. *Regroup* ideas.	*Metacognitive processes and critical analysis:* Ask students to regroup their ideas based on a reanalysis of their views. Remind them to use their metacognitive processing skills, experiences, and a variety of resources. They must explain why they made the choices they made.
6. *Connect* and *synthesize* ideas.	*Critical analysis/extending content:* Instruct students to connect these ideas to their own experiences and prior ideas, and to relate them back to science content standards. Use their ideas to establish a baseline of points for connecting future science activities to what students see as science, and determine and build on student understandings and experiences.

Concept Attainment Model of Instruction

Like the concept formation model, *concept attainment* focuses on attaining science concepts. However, unlike concept formation, during which students provide and shape input, during concept attainment you give examples and "nonexamples" that students use to determine a broad concept or idea. This model allows you to introduce vocabulary

. . . .●

55

and concepts that are unfamiliar to students in a way that diminishes anxiety. Indeed, many teachers demonstrate this teaching model in a way that evokes play or games. When students understand how the "game" is played, encourage them to create their own examples/nonexamples and to ask their classmates to help them define the bigger concept related to the examples provided. This model of teaching enhances students' thinking skills and concept development. Specific steps for the concept attainment model are listed in Table 4.2 along with a sample lesson plan.

TABLE 4.2 Concept Attainment Model

1. Provide *examples* of a concept or idea. Next, provide *nonexamples* of the same concept. Then, ask for student input.	*Scaffolding/discourse:* Before beginning the lesson, indicate the purpose of the lesson: to learn what a concept is and what it is not. Teach students the difference between examples and nonexamples. Provide examples and nonexamples before asking for student input. For example, you could hold up multiple images of a biome from another continent along with several nonexamples of distinct biomes not supported on that continent. When possible, select a biome from a continent that includes the native countries of your students.
2. Provide additional ideas without divulging whether they are examples or nonexamples.	*Redistributing authority/scaffolding/extending content:* Instruct students to use their prior knowledge (including discussions with other students) and resources to determine whether the ideas you have presented are examples or nonexamples of the concept. Consider adding images of the people who live in these biomes, traditional shelters, and any other identifying markers. Include nonexamples as well. Ask students to talk about what they think the pictures of the biome represent, whether it is familiar to them, and what they know about the particular biome. Include pictures of flora and fauna that live in the biome and those that do not.

(Continued)

Integrating Cognitive Views of Learning

TABLE 4.2 Concept Attainment Model (*Continued*)

3. Tell students to create their own examples and nonexamples (in small groups, if appropriate).	*Metacognitive processes and critical thinking:* Instruct students to use examples in their own lives to come up with additional examples and nonexamples. Ask them how they came up with these examples, on what prior knowledge they are building, and how these examples relate to their own experiences.
	Have students write and draw additional examples and nonexamples of the biome that is the focal point of the discussion. Let them know that they can augment their drawings or writings by detailing their experiences with the biome under study (for example, when they visited this or a similar biome).

Inquiry Models

As discussed in Chapters 1 and 2, inquiry-based learning encourages students to take more responsibility for their learning because *they* pursue science knowledge. They ask science-related questions, determine ways of answering these questions (holding authority in the classroom temporarily), and interpret (and even challenging) findings. With inquiry-based learning, the *group investigation model* encourages cooperative group work to solve problems; the *learning cycle model* encourages exploration in small groups or individually.

Group Investigation

A group investigation lesson places students at the center of the activities. Together, students collaborate with their peers to inquire into, solve, and generate a better understanding of science problems and content. Based on particular science activities, experiments, or readings, students determine and generate specific questions they then try to answer. Your role is one of a facilitator; you support students' capacity to investigate and understand scientific phenomena (derived from or connected to the science content standards). (Background information and examples related to inquiry and science inquiry processes were presented in Chapter 2.) The six different phases of the group investigation model are described in Table 4.3.

TABLE 4.3 Group Investigation Model

Puzzlement: Begin with what students are familiar with and spin it to provoke interest. For example, let's return to that *ceviche* we discussed in an earlier chapter. Use lemon and fish to provoke a discussion on the denaturation process. Saturate a white fish with lemon and have students conduct observations in the classroom for a period of several hours.	*Redistributing authority/connecting to homes/encouraging conversations/ developing independent thinking:* You or your students provide a puzzling situation. This is more authentic when a real problem arises during a science activity. For example, when second-grade students are observing a variety of organisms in a saltwater aquarium, they may see things that puzzle them and they may want to ask questions about them.
1. *Ask questions:* Have students write questions and draw pictures that reflect what they see happening with the fish soaked in lemon.	*Redistributing authority:* Students ask questions related to their observations and puzzlements.
2. *Group formation:* Beginning in dyads and moving into heterogeneous groups, have students determine which *ceviche* questions they can answer by observation, by touching the fish, by smelling the fish, and so on.	*Redistributing authority/developing independent thinking:* Students take the initiative to determine which questions can be answered. You facilitate and scaffold this process when necessary. Have students divide into groups according to specific questions.
3. *Group investigation:* Have students investigate the ways in which the lemon has changed the structure of the fish over time. Ask them to note what sorts of changes have occurred in relation to what they can see, feel, and smell each hour of study.	*Redefining responsibilities/encouraging real conversations/developing independent thinking:* Students work in their groups to answer questions through a variety of resources and additional activities or experiments, or by making additional observations and recording answers. They can challenge information provided by their own observations, references, and experiences.
4. *Group monitoring:* Ensure student responsibilities are equitably distributed within each group and that roles rotate from activity to activity so no student is always relegated to one role.	*Scaffolding content/redistributing authority:* Use scaffolding techniques to ask students questions to help them think more critically or to assist them if they are "stuck" on a particular area of the investigation.

(Continued)

Inquiry Models

TABLE 4.3 Group Investigation Model (*Continued*)

5. *Group presentations:* Ensure students have opportunities to present information orally and visually. Invite family members to watch or participate in presentations.	*Redistribution of authority/nurturing positive attitudes:* Students make presentations to their peers in ways they choose and determine is appropriate. The group decides whether to create a PowerPoint presentation, act out a play to describe their findings, or present their findings in another way. **FAMILY** **CONNECTIONS**
6. *Group evaluation and recycling:* Provide students with a rubric that asks them to evaluate their roles in the process and presentation of learning.	*Redistribute authority/metacognitive processes/critical analysis/extending content:* Students evaluate their learning and answers to questions, ask new questions, and then recycle any questions that need greater scrutiny.

The 5 Es Instructional Model

The 5 Es instructional model was adapted from the learning cycle model that has been used for many years to promote inquiry and to enhance scientific understanding. The learning cycle model has three main phases: explore, explain, and apply. The 5 E model extends the learning cycle model to engage, explore, explain, elaborate, and evaluate. During the first step, you engage students by creating excitement and curiosity. Next, you give students a variety of objects, pictures, or other items to explore freely. The third step involves explaining as students communicate with each other; you serve as a facilitator to challenge students' ideas. The fourth step is when students discuss their ideas and puzzlements, and determine overarching science concepts or big ideas. In addition, students apply new vocabulary, new explanations, and relate their previous knowledge to new knowledge. During the final step, students evaluate and reflect on their understanding and new knowledge. The steps are listed and described in Table 4.4.

TABLE 4.4 The 5 Es Instructional Model

1. *Engage:* Bring to the classroom photos that you've taken in the school neighborhood. Include storm drains, rain gutters, puddles, reservoirs, open water tanks, and any other sites where water collects or flows.	*Nurturing positive attitudes/connecting to home lives:* Create interest, present a puzzling situation, incite curiosity in your students based on things with which they are familiar, but with which they have *not* connected to science processes in school. Ask questions—and encourage students to ask questions—about an object, picture, video clip, or demonstration related to the example described on the left.
2. *Explore:* Move students into the field (for example, the schoolyard, the local neighborhood) to examine similar water-related sites. Prompt students to list, illustrate, and describe any and all characteristics of these sites. Have them explore in pairs (partner ELLs with more English-proficient peers).	*Redistributing authority/developing independent thinking:* Students conduct local observations of similar water-related sites (on campus or off campus, depending on time, space, and safety contingencies). Encourage them to write and draw examples of similar sites, and to record their descriptions and ideas in their native or target language.
3. *Explain:* Ask student pairs to explain their water-related sites to other pairs, prompting what are now small groups to represent their "joint" findings in Venn diagrams.	*Encouraging real conversation/scaffolding content/metacognitive processes:* Students work together to generate explanations or to communicate their ideas related to their explorations. Facilitate students' formation of explanations by asking them questions, challenging their thinking, and instructing groups to compare their ideas. At this point, you can begin to assist students in applying scientific labels to some of their ideas.
4. *Elaborate:* Ask newly formed groups of four students to hypothesize what happens to water collected in these sites. Where does the water go if it is contained? If it is not contained (for example, it runs into a storm drain or sewer), where does the water flow? Is the flow obstructed? Unobstructed? What affects the collection and/or flow of water at the site they are examining?	*Discourse/extending and connecting content:* Students apply their new knowledge and experiences by asking additional questions, setting up additional experiments or activities, and connecting their school science learning with examples from their home or neighborhood, and they use new vocabulary.

(Continued)

TABLE 4.4 The 5 Es Instructional Model (*Continued*)

5. *Evaluate:* Have group representatives canvass other groups to share and collect information. Ask all representatives to return to their "home" group with information from at least two other groups. Direct the groups to evaluate their new information and to create a graphic organizer that reflects information they determined was the most compelling.	*Extending and connecting content:* Students use metacognition strategies to think and reflect about their own learning. They assess their understanding of the science content, ask additional questions, and compare their previous ideas with their new knowledge. Students can take what they discovered about water-related sites in their neighborhood and can look for information about water collection and transit in their textbook or in other resources. Students can also compare the sites in their neighborhood with others. Are drains clogged? Dirty? Free flowing? Where does the water end up?

Child inquiring outside.

FAMILY

CONNECTIONS

Making Models of Teaching More Culturally Relevant

Culturally relevant teaching strategies and models can be integrated into every area of the science curriculum. It is important to include families in homework assignments and other science activities whenever possible. Families, their culture, and their experiences should be considered as value-added resources when helping students learn science. A variety of concept development strategies and models, inquiry models, and action-based science learning can enhance science for *all* students. It is important to remember that the most culturally relevant instruction starts and ends with students. What do they understand coming into your classroom? How can you build on their experiences? How can you use the community as a site of science inquiry? Seeing what *is* there, as opposed to what *is* not, will establish a foundation for instruction that is both reflective of students' cultures *and* relevant to their lives.

. . . .

61

CASE STUDY   Teachers and Students Participating in a Group Investigation Science Activity

Mr. Murray starts class by sharing a disagreement he had with Ms. Kenta, a teacher at another school located in the more affluent, surrounding suburbs. Ms. Kenta had just initiated a special ecology project using the lush yard at her school site and was sharing details of the project with Mr. Murray. When she commented it was a shame that Mr. Murray's students couldn't do ecological studies in their schoolyard because of their urban setting and lack of biodiversity, Mr. Murray got upset. He was not sure he agreed with this.

"So class," he added, after sharing this story with his students, "I've decided this is going to be the project for our ecology unit. What do you think about what Ms. Kenta said? Do you agree with her?"

Students started to raise their hands, but Mr. Murray explained they would start the discussion by working in groups. He added that, rather than just sharing their opinions, Mr. Murray expected each group to come up with a plan for exploring this issue. Earlier in the year they had studied the importance of collecting data to support conclusions, and Mr. Murray was building on these experiences now with something that hit close to home—*very* close. How could they go about exploring the different plants and animals that inhabited their urban schoolyard? How would they define biodiversity where they lived?

"That's not an easy question!" exclaimed one of the students. "It will take a lot longer than one class period to do that."

"Looks like you have already identified one of the resources you'll need for your investigation. Time. What else would be important to consider in planning our investigation?" Mr. Murray asked.

The students huddled over their desks. Some groups elected one person to be the recorder whereas others took notes in their own folders. Some mentioned the importance of starting with a research question; others decided doing an observational survey could be the focus of the investigation. One boy suggested that his father, a landscaper, was an expert they could consult to help them identify different plant species. One girl mentioned that her sister had a book about local birds and that she could probably borrow it from her sister. Some students argued there wasn't anything but cement on the school grounds and a single, half-dead tree. Another noted that his lunch was attacked every day by gulls. Many students noted that they all avoided the PE shed because they didn't like all the spiders.

Students quickly realized there were many opinions in their group. Mr. Murray circulated among them, providing management guidance, but leaving the planning to the students. Just before the end of the class period, he called for their attention.

"We are going to spend the rest of this week planning the process we can use to make an ecological survey of our schoolyard. You can choose to use the Internet to explore published studies about different methods or you can read through some of the science journals on my bookshelf. You can even share ideas between groups or simply focus on an original method. On Friday, we'll have each group share their plan."

"Do we get to *do* the study then or are we just talking about it?" shouted out an especially eager student.

Mr. Murray smiled and commented, "It wouldn't be an investigation if we just sat around talking about it would it?"

After the bell, students filed out to their next class. They were already talking about how exciting it would be to spend time outside the classroom conducting a study of their own schoolyard. They hadn't realized that it could be a wildlife habitat despite its location—in the heart of the city.

Reflecting on the Case

1. How did Mr. Murray empower his students?

2. How did Mr. Murray encourage group investigation to understand the science of their local ecosystem?

2. How could Mr. Murray improve his lesson to provide more culturally relevant aspects?

• Book Study Questions •

1. What models of instruction do you think would be most useful in your science classroom? Explain why.

2. Consider the model with which you're most comfortable. What would you need to do to integrate more culturally relevant instruction, as in the examples?

3. How can you integrate students' interest into science instruction? Where can you inquire into their interests to determine instructional "next steps?"

4. How can some of the instructional strategies help your ELLs become more confident in understanding science and doing science?

5. How can you be most helpful with students when they are working on cooperative group projects and activities?

6. How can you teach students about the value of creativity in science?

• References and Suggested Readings •

Delgado-Gaitan, C. (2004). *Involving Latino families in schools: Raising student achievement through home–school partnerships.* Thousand Oaks, CA: Corwin Press.

Fisher, A. (2001). *An introduction to critical thinking.* Cambridge: Cambridge University Press.

Hartman, H. J. (1998). Metacognition in teaching and learning: An introduction. *Instructional Science, 26,* 1–3.

Lave, J., & Wenger, E. (1991). *Situated learning: Legitimate peripheral participation.* Cambridge: Cambridge University Press.

Puccio, G. J., & Murdock, M. C. (2001). Creative thinking: An essential life skill. In A. Costa, *Developing minds: A source book for teaching thinking* (pp. 67–71). Alexandria, VA: ASCD.

Schunk, D. H. (2008). *Learning theories: An educational perspective.* 5th ed. Upper Saddle River, NJ: Pearson.

Vygotsky, L. S. (1978). *Mind in society: The development of higher psychological processes.* Ed., Trans. M. Cole, V. John-Steiner, S. Scribner & E. Souberman. Boston, MA: Harvard University Press.

Westheimer, J., & Kahne, J. (2004). What kind of citizen? The politics of educating for democracy. *American Educational Research Journal, 41,* 237–269.

Assessment and Evaluation, and Culturally and Linguistically Diverse Students

• Prior Knowledge and Beliefs Organizer •

- What is a grade (for example, on a test or a homework assignment)?
- What are the best ways to collect information and determine students' grades (for example, in science achievement, conceptual understanding, or interest in science)?

Consider your answers to the questions above as you read about the various assessment strategies described in this chapter. It is important to remember that our personal views can influence grading and how we determine students' achievement. *How* we collect information and the *types* of information we collect are critical to determining students' actual achievement in science. Thus, we need to acknowledge that what we collect and—just as important—what we do not collect affect the ways we teach and how we provide access to science for all our students. Assessing students in multiple ways ensures students have a variety of opportunities to show what they know and the degrees to which they understand concepts or can apply skills. Conducting assessments in only one way may be great for some children, but it will leave other students out, even if they know a great deal about the content.

Multidimensional Assessment

In this chapter we examine multiple assessment measures to determine which are more suited for specific tasks and which provide opportunities for all students to show what they know and what they can do. In addition, we focus on *assessment*, not evaluation. Evaluation is a fine way to make decisions about students' learning and progress at particular, predetermined end points, but assessment—unlike evaluation—is used to shape the unfolding teaching and learning dynamic in each classroom. When you assess students' work, attitudes, or skills, you are collecting information that you will use to shape instruction. In contrast, when you evaluate students' work, attitudes, or skills, you are making a decision or judgment about what students have learned, before moving on to other topics or content.

Thus, although it is clear that assessment and evaluation are related, it is just as clear that they are not the same thing. *Assessment* involves the regular collection of information about students' strengths, challenges, and needs to inform teaching and learning. *Evaluation* consists of making a judgment or decision based on what students show on particular assignments, during certain activities, or on specific tests. Assessment is used to gauge students' understanding, skill development, and attitude related to science, whereas evaluation is used to determine whether students have met grade-level standards or performed in a prespecified manner on a text-based test or standardized test. We focus on assessment in this chapter because assessment is responsive and formative. Assessment can be teacher designed and/or student designed, and it allows for students to be part of the process. It can also be used to provide information for students, teachers, and families that enhances learning, because it is more reflective of specific, dynamic, and in-the-moment instructional growth. Stiggins (2008) highlights four components that are important in the design of high-quality assessment for all students. These involve considering the following:

1. *Why we assess*
   - Understanding the purpose of the assessment
   - Recognizing for whom and for what purpose we will use the information

2. *What we assess*
   - Identifying specific learning outcomes
   - Ensuring the appropriateness of outcomes

3. *How we assess*
   - Creating appropriate and specific methods
   - Using quality assessment procedures

4. *How we communicate the assessment and information gained*

- Identifying to whom the assessment is reported
- Determining in what form the assessment is reported
- Deciding how the assessment is reported

Keeping Stiggins's (2008) components in mind as we design instruction and corresponding assessments helps to ensure that these two dimensions are integrated and that we are paying attention to the characteristics of our classrooms while meeting science standards. This is particularly important because cultural mismatches between teaching and learning exist for many students, especially ELLs or those from diverse backgrounds. Traditional written tests are even more problematic for students from non-English backgrounds, because written tests are so dependent on English proficiency.

Different Assessment Methods

There are various forms of assessment methods to help you collect information about your students, what they know, and what they can do. Some of the most effective methods for science include portfolios, products, performances, and attitude surveys. These are all viable alternatives to the traditional written tests and assignments that remain the primary testing mechanisms in science classrooms today. This chapter discusses written tests that provide opportunities for students to be more successful on state-mandated tests, but for the most part this chapter focuses on alternative assessment methods that are more appropriate for diverse students.

Considering a culturally relevant approach based on Ladson-Billings' (1995) three components of culturally relevant instruction, you should keep the following in mind when collecting information and determining assessment methods: high academic success, cultural competence, and critical consciousness. Table 5.1 outlines these three areas and provides examples of culturally relevant assessments.

TABLE 5.1 Culturally Relevant Assessment Procedures

High academic success	• Assess the same science standards for *all* students • Focus on assessing for student success rather than trying to "trick" students or making assessment a "mystery" • Provide multiple assessment methods for the same science standards • Embed assessment in science activities when feasible (For example, when students are creating a poster that shows different classes of animals, assess their understanding by examining the poster rather than creating an additional quiz or other assignment.) • Allow students to use Flip video cameras or audiotapes to reflect on their learning and to record what they are learning, or to demonstrate the application of science skills (incorporating their native language when appropriate)
Cultural competence	• Include students' strengths and experiences to assess what they know and can do • Include students' prior experiences at home and in their neighborhood in science activities and assessment • Ensure your assessments consider things from multiple perspectives • Have students rotate into regularly changing, diverse small groups (sharing information and distributing responsibilities) • Ask open-ended, process-focused questions
Critical consciousness	• Include students in creating the assessment process/instrument: rubrics, criteria, assessment methods • Allow time for students to examine their work and reflect on their progress and understanding or development of science skills via portfolios • Encourage students to gain power through knowledge of the use of appropriate resources such as books, media, and other resources • Encourage students to compare different sources of knowledge and information in a variety of resources beyond the textbook, such as primary sources or science Internet sources • Have students tackle real-world issues using science • Assess group projects by considering content comprehension and group collaboration

Different Assessment Methods

Products

Products are easily embedded in science activities. Products can take the form of journal entries, drawings, concept maps, circle maps, science reports, science video newscasts, or other "tangibles" that relate to science content knowledge and understanding. Using products, students show how well they have developed an understanding of specific science content. When thoughtfully designed, products can reflect how students apply scientific knowledge. Asking students to reflect on the product and the process of creating the product can also tap into their feelings about the science involved, as well as aid in developing their capacities to express themselves—two components important in the design of a more culturally relevant way of assessing.

Student's poster of a fish camouflaged in its environment.

In general, and traditionally, products focus on knowledge. Stiggins (2008) warns, however, that knowledge only goes so far; knowing something is not the same thing as understanding it. He argues that when students figure out how their new knowledge fits into their broader life and experiences, they then gain true understanding. This supports our efforts to design assessments that are culturally relevant. Stiggins's (2008) assertion highlights the importance of developing connections between the science students learn in school and their experiences outside of school.

When participating in science activities or experiments (note that activities related to science content and experiments include specific tasks, such as controlling variables), allow students to make decisions based on a collection of evidence rather than following a step-by-step adult-created science format.

Students can gain knowledge and develop independent science authority as they select and determine which resources are most appropriate for specific tasks. Products that reflect real issues and, in particular, issues students can recognize (such as bar graphs that compare locations of city or state parks with communities, and the prevalence of types of flora and fauna in each) will help students make links between school science and science in their neighborhood and community.

Journal Entries

Science notebooks or journals are another way to assess students' understanding and ability to communicate their ideas. In science journals, students can write; create tables, charts, and drawings; or use other means to demonstrate their understanding. Journals and notebooks are an authentic way of assessing students' science ideas because their use mirrors what real scientists do when they are asking questions and collecting information to answer their questions. Inviting scientists of diverse ethnic backgrounds to talk about and show their notebooks can further support students' understanding of the role journals, notebooks, and writing in general play in science, as well as provide students with exposure to the possibilities science holds for people "just like them."

Students can use science journals to

- Record their observations or collect information over time
- Reflect on their learning
- Record their science-related questions and possible ways to locate answers
- Make connections between science in their neighborhood and homes with science at school

You can provide feedback by reading your students' entries and writing on "sticky" notes or other paper to comment on students' writings, content, and questions. In addition, encourage students to read each other's journals and to provide questions, comments, and other helpful feedback. Be sure you let students know from the beginning what you are looking for in their journals. For example, do not explicitly assess students' use of grammar in their journals (do this during some science assignments, but not journals). Focus, instead, on content, process, and individual growth. This will make at least one dimension of science assessment less linguistically threatening to those students who are still developing their English proficiency.

Drawings

Based on the maxim that *a picture is worth a thousand words,* drawings often reveal more information than written responses or other traditional measures, particularly in the case of ELLs. Students from non-English language backgrounds can often draw their ideas with greater competence than when assessed via written formats, because they needn't struggle with the complexities of language. Student drawings, therefore, can serve as a means to assess concept comprehension, integrated knowledge, connections to student experiences, and even misconceptions students may have.

One of the strengths of using student drawings as an assessment method is that you can compare and contrast students' understanding over time (Cox-Petersen & Olson, 2007). Using drawing as a preassessment at the beginning of a science unit, during the middle of a science unit, at the immediate end of a science unit, or even later in the school year provides you with valuable information about student learning over time.

Cox-Petersen and Olson (2007) share an example of how they assessed students' understanding of the ocean at four points (September, November, March, and June) during an eight-month period. On each occasion, students were provided with plain white paper and given the same verbal prompt: "Draw a picture of what is in the ocean, using as much detail as possible." Students were then given four types of scores to assess their understanding of different areas of the ocean. The first score reflected the total number of unique animals present in the drawing. The second score included the total number of unique plants. The third score included the total number of unique nonliving features, such as sea mounts, volcanoes, trenches, and so on. A fourth score reflected the level of sophistication of the drawing, using a rubric ranging from 0 to 5 points (*sophistication* refers to the accuracy of the placement of living organisms and how well the drawing reflected an understanding of major marine science concepts). The following rubric was used to determine sophistication scores: 0 point, no drawing or a drawing of one organism and the water surface; 1 point, two or more animals and water surface; 2 points, plants or the ocean floor and two or more animals; 3 points, swimming and stationary animals, plants, and ocean floor; 4 points, ocean floor with features, swimming and stationary animals, plants, and most are placed accurately; 5 points, extensive ocean floor features with appropriate organisms, many animals and plants, and accurate placement, and shows some relationships between organisms (for example, a whale with baleen eating krill). Four different scores allowed teachers to examine the depth and breadth of understanding related to plants, animals, ocean features, and the interaction of organisms in their marine environment. The rubric provided clear expectations for students at the beginning of the assignment and encouraged high academic success.

Coupling drawings with additional forms of assessment such as interviews or other products provides an even more holistic measure of understanding. Indeed, as discussed at the beginning of this chapter, designing multiple forms of assessment provides for and secures the means to access more of our students' understandings of science. No one way will show as much as multiple forms of assessment can.

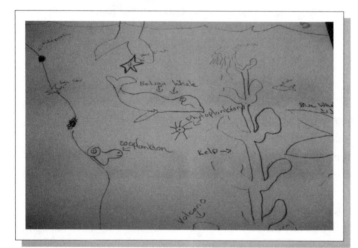

Student drawing of the ocean.

Concept Maps

In Chapter 3 you read about the power of concept maps in illustrating students' understanding of concepts. Concept maps are helpful to you when assessing students'

- Prior knowledge
- Science conceptions and misconceptions
- Personal organization of scientific ideas

Using concepts maps, students generate ideas and show characteristics or connections among science concepts by drawing lines from the center of the page to other areas. As discussed earlier, you must teach students *how* to create concept maps, show them examples of different types of concept maps, and provide lots of time for students to practice creating concept maps. Students can record their ideas in their native language (when appropriate) and show the ways in which they have organized their own understanding of science concepts and terms. Providing visuals to go along with terms will further assist ELLs and other students unfamiliar with scientific language.

Science Reports

Science reports are much more than handwritten essays. They can include PowerPoint presentations, posters, or other means of conveying understanding of a particular science topic or topics. When students prepare science reports, they should be allowed some choice of topics related to the science content standards. Here are some helpful steps to keep in mind when assigning a science report:

1. Have students determine a topic of their choice based on the topic of study and content standards.
2. Next, request students to list a variety of questions that they are curious about related to that topic.
3. Then, instruct students to determine which questions will yield more information before they use a variety of resources to locate answers to their questions. Be specific about the types of resources they need to include.
4. Last, tell students that they are responsible for determining a way to present their answers in narrative form. Also, they must figure out ways to organize their information, such as in different categories or within each question.

When possible, allow students to work in groups on science reports. Ensure responsibilities and abilities are fairly distributed. For example, partner ELLs with more proficient students, better researchers with those less so, artists with those less confident, and ethnic and class minority students with those from the majority. This allows students to develop relationships with one another, build on one another's skills, and further support English language acquisition as ELLs interact with their more proficient peers.

Performances

Performances are mostly skill related and are based on students actually doing something such as using a microscope, conducting experiments, working in cooperative groups, measuring items, or participating in interviews and discussions. Science activities and experiments, cooperative group work, and oral presentations can be designed as culturally relevant ways to assess students' skill and performance. Researchers do caution, however, that the mere act of changing the assessment method does not ensure bias-free assessment related to students' cultural and language backgrounds (Garcia & Pearson, 1994; Shaw, 1997). What can make these types of assessments culturally relevant is a consideration of what was taught, how it was taught, and whether and how we connected and scaffolded instruction relative to students' understanding and experience when we assess in these ways.

Performance assessments and products can be more appropriate measures of student learning with regard to ethnically and culturally diverse students—for example, when they spring directly from instructional activities. In this way, these types of assessments can explicitly build on what is taught, scaffolded as part of the whole process of learning, and formatively and responsively developed as instruction progresses. This keeps the teaching and learning dynamic much more tightly connected and responsive to particular students' needs, understandings, and experiences. Of course, no matter the assessment mechanism selected, each assessment measure must be scrutinized to ensure equity and access to high academic performance for all students.

Experiments, Group Work, and Presentations

Teachers can gain a lot of insight into students' feelings and understandings of science when observing students actually "doing" science, whether it be an experiment during which they are asking questions, controlling variables, and finding answers, or whether they are observing different types of marine fossils, comparing the adequacy of different types of shelters in different parts of the world, or examining the nutritional content in foods common to particular cultures. You can create a checklist or other way to record students' performance, participation, and progress during specific tasks (see Table 5.2).

TABLE 5.2 Student Group Work and Self-Assessment

Student	Name three things that your group learned from the activity	Name two things that your group did well	Name two things that your group could improve on
Maria			
Hsing Chi			
Abraham			

Interviews and Discussions

Interviews provide yet another means of assessing science content and process understandings. In preparation for interviews, either you, the students, or everyone together
can create a list of interview questions relevant to the science topic under study that
allows students to show, orally, their understanding of the particular subject. For example,
students can create a list of questions they would like to ask you or other students related
to specific science content. This creates a reciprocal process in which everyone has the
power to gain valuable information about science, because coming up with questions
about the topic depends on some consideration of the topic. Taking this a step further,
whenever a student is "stumped" by a question, they can use a variety of resources to
check for the answer.

Interviews should be comfortable, and students should feel safe and secure when
discussing their ideas. During interviews, ask questions that relate to science content and
that reflect students' language and culture. When possible, allow students to be inter-
viewed in pairs or to interview each other in teams. Once again, this provides a supportive
mechanism for including ELLs in what might otherwise be a linguistically exclusionary
activity. During interviews, your role is one of active listener, and you provide feedback
to students, thus building on and cultivating their interest in and understanding of science.

Portfolios

Portfolios include student-selected samples of their own work. This immediately transfers
some degree of authority of knowledge to the students, because they must decide which
particular samples to incorporate into their portfolio and describe why they have selected
them to represent their progress and development in science. Samples can include products such as essays, experiment logs, drawings, journals, or concept maps, or performances such as group work evaluations or videotapes of presentations. The purpose of
a portfolio is for students to take an active part in critically analyzing and demonstrating
their learning and achievement via the creation of a showcase that reflects a range of their
work. Encourage students to reflect on their learning and choose artifacts that will show
what they know and can do, and make sure they include several different types of work.

Students can write, tape, or illustrate their reflections about their work and learning.
Audiotapes or videotapes are an efficient way for students to discuss their artifacts, to
describe what they have gained through the instructional process, and to identify goals
for future portfolios. Taping is culturally relevant, because students reflect on what they
are learning, their perceptions of their own learning, and how well they are demonstrating their understanding of science concepts and skills—as *they* understand it. Again,
the students determine what they express. In addition, on tape, students are able to
discuss their performance in lieu of writing, a task that is often more difficult for some

students (and may inhibit a true reflection for some ELLs). Portfolios, therefore, place the responsibility on the student to assess their actual science performance and then share their achievement with you, their families, and other students. Some teachers and students enjoy showcasing portfolios like one would an art exhibit, where families can enjoy snacks and walk around the room or other area to observe what students know and can do in science. Inviting families to bring in traditional foods from their cultures for the science showcase (if your school allows this) can be another way of connecting the importance of science to home lives.

FAMILY
CONNECTIONS

You may want to help students organize their portfolios according to the science content standards for their state. In this way, students show how they meet the standards. If, moreover, you have scaffolded standards-based instruction in relation to students' experiences, built assessments into a range of activities, and provided a variety of assessment mechanisms as described throughout this book, then the artifacts that go into any student's portfolio will better connect with central tenets of culturally relevant instruction. A true culturally relevant approach depends on these components to ensure students meet high academic standards that are consistent with state-mandated content and skills. Thus, a culturally relevant approach to assessment builds on what exists (student experiences and understanding) in the pursuit of what can be (science-savvy students from all backgrounds). This is particularly important in an era focused on standardized tests. Ensuring we align culturally relevant instruction with science content standards for specific grade levels means recognizing the role standardized tests play in all our students' ultimate academic access and opportunities.

Teachers can help to facilitate the inquiry process.

Assessing Attitudes, Values, and Beliefs

Science knowledge and skills are at the forefront of assessment, whereas the assessment of students' attitudes, values, and beliefs are usually ignored. Although students' feelings about science are some of the most important indicators and predictors of learning and motivation to learn, they remain one of the most neglected areas of assessment in schools.

In Chapter 3 we discussed how motivation to learn affects achievement. Thus, we want to be sure to address the need to assess and to consider students' ongoing feelings about science as they unfold in our classrooms. Student attitudes toward science are important at every grade level when optimizing high academic achievement. In addition, students must have a purpose for learning science, and be able to relate science content and skills to other aspects of their lives. Some culturally relevant ways to assess students' attitudes include drawings, home visits, surveys, classroom events, and activities. Assessing students' dispositions—which include attitudes, values, and beliefs—can be done formally through surveys or informally through drawings, observations, or classroom discussions. Building opportunities for reflection into every science unit, via written or drawn documents, will help teachers get a regular reading of their students' feelings. Over time, too, these student reflections on science processes can aid you in designing subsequent instruction. By regularly reviewing student reflections, you can rapidly identify particular points at which students are struggling and/or succeeding in science, and use them to modify subsequent activities.

Drawings and Surveys

Just as teachers can gauge student understanding by using drawings as products, drawings can also be used to collect information about students' attitudes, beliefs, and other ideas about science and science content. In addition, surveys are useful to gauge students' views and attitudes. This is true particularly if the surveys are anonymous. Although you will not be able to match the survey with the student, you can gain powerful insight into general trends in the classroom.

When creating a survey, determine the specific information you would like to collect from your students. Inform them that the survey will not be graded, but that you are collecting information to find out about what they like, don't like, or would like more of in science. Questions should be concise and should avoid difficult vocabulary or jargon to ensure that all students are able to provide their ideas and input. Multiple-choice surveys are popular because they are easy to assess, but open-ended surveys that require students to provide varied responses sometimes yield more in-depth information. Thus, include both types of questions on your survey. For young children, teachers often use faces with smiles, no expression, or frowns to allow students to express their attitudes about particular science topics when survey questions are read orally.

Alternative Parent–Teacher Conferences

Parent–teacher conferences have been a long-lived tradition in many schools across the United States. Most of the time, the teacher talks and the parents listen. To provide a more culturally relevant parent–teacher conference, this tradition must change in some ways. The student-led conferences discussed in Chapter 6 are an effective way to include students in self-assessment and in communicating their achievement and progress. In addition, work with students to determine the most appropriate ways to conduct conferences that involve them.

Assessing Portfolios, Products, and Performances

After students have participated in products, performances, and the creation of portfolios, their academic success and progress must be assessed based on specific criteria. The use of rubrics, peer reviews, self-reviews, observations, and interviews are all appropriate ways to assess. Using a variety of these assessment tools allows for more opportunities for students to demonstrate their understanding and skills. Clearly showing students how rubrics are designed based on what was taught further helps them understand the relationship of instruction and assessment, increases their understanding of the metacognitive processes in assessment, and helps them see how assessments are fair and equitable.

CASE STUDY   Mrs. Weirath's Garden

The following case study includes quotes from students in Mrs. Weirath's kindergarten class. Many of her students are ELLs and have had little experience growing plants or tending to a garden. During April and May, Mrs. Weirath provided a variety of experiences for her students to plan, plant, maintain, and observe a class garden. The following are a series of quotes from her students.

"Ladybugs are really good for the plants and worms. They help the plants grow. I planted beets and they are growing a lot!" —Elizabeth

"Corn, radishes, beets, cucumbers, and potatoes are growing in the monkey garden. Water, ladybugs, worms, soil stuff, and butterflies help the garden grow." —Jude

"You need water, soil, seeds, sun, and air for the flowers to grow. I think the corn is going to grow all the way to the moon!" —Juan

"I planted corn because I love eating it. I want to eat it when it's done growing. I want to plant some at home too." —Ainsley

"I planted a cucumber and I think it's going to be as long as my arm." —Miley

"You have to put ladybugs in the garden so they can eat the bugs. Every time you have to water them a little so they don't die. I want to eat a beet when it's done." —Ethan

"A garden needs a lot of sun so the flowers bloom in the summer." —Henry

"We put the ladybugs in the garden to eat the aphids. I planted the corn." —Ido

"We had to pull weeds, plant and dig and water our garden. Now it looks pretty. I like the Ninja Monkey garden. I can't wait to eat the corn." —Nic

"The tomatoes are growing very tall. There are yellow flowers that will turn into tomatoes. They need water and sun and air to grow." —Bee

"We learned that the sunflowers need water, the corn needs lots of water. The plants like the ladybugs because they will help them grow." —Arturo

Reflecting on the Case

1. What can you infer about how Mrs. Weirath incorporated her students' prior knowledge into the garden activity (based on the student quotes)?

2. What can you determine about student learning based on these quotes?

3. What attitudes and affective measures can be assessed from the student quotes?

• Book Study Questions •

1. What are the advantages and disadvantages of using multiple forms of assessment?

2. How will you get a more accurate picture of what students know and what they can do by including a variety of assessment measures such as drawings, concept maps, and student products?

3. What new assessment strategies would you consider using in your classroom?

4. Why would it be important for students to help create a rubric for a science assignment or have knowledge of a teacher-created rubric before completing a project?

5. How can students help to assess their own understanding of science?

6. How can you help students assess their own understanding of science?

• References and Suggested Readings •

Costa, V. (1995). When science is "another world": Relationships between family, friends, school, and science. *Science Education, 79,* 313–333.

Cox-Petersen, A. (2010). *Educational partnerships: Connecting schools, families, and the community.* Los Angeles, CA: Sage.

Cox-Petersen, A., & Olson, J. K. (2007). Alternative assessments for English language learners: Using drawings and interviews to measure student learning. *Science and Children, 44,* 46–48.

Garcia, G. E., & Pearson, P. D. (1994). Assessment and diversity. In *Review of research in education,* ed. L. Darling-Hammond (pp. 337–391). Washington, DC: American Educational Research Association.

Ladson-Billings, G. (1995). But that's just good

teaching! The case for culturally relevant pedagogy. *Theory Into Practice, 34,* 159–165.

Moll, L. C. (1997). Teachers as social scientists:
Learning about culture from household research.
In *Race, ethnicity and multiculturalism. Vol. 1,* ed.
P. M. Hall (pp. 89–114). New York: Garland.

Moll, L. C., Velez-Ibanez, C., Greenberg, J., &
Rivera, C. (1990). *Community knowledge and
classroom practice: Combining resources for
literacy instruction.* Arlington, VA: Development
Associates.

Patchen, T., Cox-Petersen, A., Ambrose, K., DeVore, A.,
& Koenings, N. (2008, March). *Teachers engaging
in informal learning experiences in students' homes.*
Presented at the annual meeting of the American Educational Research Association, New York, NY.

Shaw, J. M. (1997). Threats to validity of science
performance assessment for English language
learners. *Journal of Research in Science Teaching,
34,* 721–743.

Stiggins, R. (2008). *Student-involved assessment for
learning.* 5th ed. Upper Saddle River, NJ: Pearson.

Family Connections

— • Prior Knowledge and Beliefs Organizer • —

- Describe three events related to science that involved your family and/or your community.

- Describe the feelings you had when you participated in science experiences with your family or community.

Consider your responses to the questions above as you read this chapter and think about providing inclusive, culturally relevant science activities that move beyond the classroom to include families and the community.

Creating New Collaborative Frameworks for Culturally Relevant Science Practices

Partnerships between families and schools have positive effects in both cognitive domains and affective domains. The cognitive domain includes knowledge and skills whereas the affective domain includes attitudes and beliefs that may influence students' overall motivation to learn. Many researchers have found that when families, communities, and schools work together in partnership, student academic achievement increases (see, for example, Epstein & Sanders [1998] and Lezotte [1997]). Indeed, Epstein (2001) found that teachers and administrators made the difference in whether families improved their knowledge about school and classroom events. Parent education level or marital status made no difference in a family's educational involvement with schools. Respecting families' values and beliefs, while encouraging them to participate as partners in their child's education, is a more contemporary perspective than the traditional role of the teacher (one who has all the knowledge and know-how).

A partnership is an agreement between two or more people or groups that work together toward shared goals. Partnerships can be formal or informal, but a partnership is most successful when both parties benefit in some way. The next section discusses families, and how schools and families can form a mutual partnership that benefits the school, community, and family.

Families

FAMILY

CONNECTIONS

The term *families* in this chapter includes parents, siblings, and extended family members who are influential in a child's life. When we think of family participation, we need to remember that for every family, their children's education is both cultural and personal. Some common themes appear in families throughout the world. Epstein (1998) conducted an international study that uncovered five main themes that recur in families and communities around the globe:

1. All families care about their children and want them to succeed in school.
2. The type of educational partnership determines who becomes involved in education and to what extent.
3. Teachers who had education and coursework related to partnerships were more successful and efficient in implementing them.
4. Collaboration is necessary to develop and sustain partnerships.
5. Consistent multinational research is needed to continue to meet the needs of families and the community to encourage broader educational partnerships.

In addition, researchers have determined three specific findings that promote educational partnerships (Cox-Petersen, 2010):

1. Children from diverse cultural backgrounds demonstrate success in formal school settings when families and teachers collaborate and make connections between the curriculum at school and at home.
2. Children perform better when their families are involved in their school and other educational activities.
3. Teachers indicate greater job satisfaction when they work in partnership with parents and other family members.

The Deficit View of Family Involvement

The deficit view of education relates to historical inequities that have negatively affected students from underrepresented groups. Essentially, the deficit view posits that when it comes to academic potential and other areas, one group is superior and other groups are inferior. This means that students who do not fit in with the majority may be found lacking because of their ethnic, social class, or linguistic backgrounds. And, generally speaking, even if they do not hold deficit views, many teachers do not consider the strengths and assets that families from diverse backgrounds offer if they focus on educating toward a specific mainstreamed culture.

Moll et al. (1990) have reported that teachers should consider inquiring and analyzing activities in students' homes to determine their strengths, because acknowledging these strengths can contribute to the academic progress of all our students in school. This view, known as *funds of knowledge,* includes thinking about the value that all families can offer a community and school. It differs from the traditional perspective that children and families, particularly those from working-class or underrepresented households, lack knowledge and experiences to be able to "add" anything to an educational partnership or curriculum. Funds of knowledge reflects an understanding that students and their families have much to offer, even if it is not recognized by the traditional, mainstream culture. By creating stronger partnerships with families, you can learn more about the knowledge that families and students offer, and use that knowledge to build bridges between students' homes and schools.

Border Crossing into Science

When students step into a science classroom, many of them feel disconnected with the content and activities, and therefore have difficulty learning or feeling as if they can actually do science. You play a crucial role in helping students cross the border between science in their home lives and science in the classroom. You can do this by making explicit connections between the science content at school and your students' culture, language, and real-life experiences.

Science can present a challenge for students from all backgrounds, but particularly for many ethnic and

Children learn firsthand about the scientific world around them.

linguistic minority students. Because students from certain cultures may be more prone to difficulties learning science and doing science than those from other cultures, it is important that you note affective dimensions (such as attitudes and beliefs, which can influence motivation) as well as cognitive ones (which relate to academic science standards). When science is presented more inclusively, students can participate in "cultural border crossing" to connect their real-life world to the science world of the classroom (Aikenhead & Jegede, 1999).

Respect for Ethnic, Linguistic, Cultural, Economic, and Educational Diversity

A respect and appreciation for students' ethnic, linguistic, cultural, economic, and educational diversity should be modeled and implemented for culturally relevant teaching and learning to take place. To do this, you (and, optimally, administrators as well) must work to overcome an unequal distribution of power related to the school–family partnerships that exist in many schools today. This unequal distribution of power happens when schools and teachers believe it is their job to "tell" parents what they should be doing or when families want to "tell" schools how they should teach. In a culturally relevant partnership model, schools and families work together to make joint educational decisions. Barton et al. (2004) describe parental participation as a dynamic, interactive process instead of a static, silent, and reserved one. They also report that involvement is not enough to engage parents, particularly those from non-English language backgrounds.

Many families from culturally and linguistically diverse backgrounds participate less in their children's educational activities because of economic and time constraints, different cultural views, and discomfort when visiting the school (Delgado-Gaitan, 2004). In addition, many immigrant families do not feel secure entering the school grounds because of their ethnic background or citizenship. However, when schools and teachers acknowledge the strengths, values, and cultural differences that exist in the different families in their school, opportunities open up for all students. By shifting the focus from what parents do to engage in their children's schooling to the hows and whys of this engagement, a more culturally relevant partnership can be achieved. This shift results in a "buy-in" on all sides as members understand and are included in decision-making processes. Parent and family experiences and actions inside and outside the school community become important factors in partnership development.

Epstein's Six Types of Involvement

Joyce Epstein (2001) defines six types of family involvement to optimize the potential for family, community, and school partnerships. By focusing on specific types of activities that encourage more family educational involvement—parenting, communication, volunteering, learning at home, decision making, and community connections—the process and outcome of teaching and learning are enhanced. Many families and schools work under the idea that participation in their child's education only takes place at the school site. In fact, many supportive educational activities can take place in the community and in homes. You, therefore, must work with families to embrace their cultural beliefs and to encourage positive educational experiences for all students.

The following lists the six types of involvement and sample activities related to teaching and learning science:

1. *Parenting* involves promoting home environments that support children's social, cognitive, emotional, and physical health. Offer parenting information to families and parents can offer information about their culture, beliefs, and educational goals for their children. Each month, send home a list of positive parenting suggestions that parents can work on with their child. Incorporate a different theme each month. For example: *During October, help your child name one fruit or vegetable that starts with each letter of the alphabet, such as* apple, bean, carrot, *and identify whether it is a fruit, root, leaf, vegetable, or other.* Or: *During April, spend at least 10 minutes with your child each day observing nature and making specific observations related to what they see, hear, and feel.* Providing information in the form of colorful inviting flyers (in various languages when appropriate) can be motivating and inviting to encourage many families to participate.

2. *Communication* involves school-to-home and home-to-school interactions. Communication can be formal or informal, monthly or weekly class newsletters, school information packets, e-mail messages, or website postings. Translate all information into languages that families can read and understand, when possible, and include visuals, too, if they will help with comprehension. Establish an open-door policy to ensure that families feel comfortable entering the school grounds, and comfortable and safe (emotionally) walking inside the classroom. Send home a weekly newsletter that outlines your current science activities and invite parents to participate in some of them.

3. *Volunteering* can take place at the school site, at home, or in the community. Ideally, encourage volunteer opportunities for all family members—mothers, fathers, cousins, aunts, uncles, grandparents, and older siblings. In addition, use family liaisons to assist in recruiting and organizing family support systems, and communicating various opportunities for volunteering and involvement. Families can volunteer their time at home by facilitating children's homework or other out-of-school science activities; by attending conferences, performances, and family events; by participating as a sports activity facilitator, recess monitor, or classroom assistant; or by becoming a member of a parent–teacher group.

4. *Learning at home* can be formal or informal. You can communicate learning activities and homework tips through regular newsletters or e-mail in a variety of languages. Science activities at home can help to prepare students for academic success in school and beyond. Some common activities involve recognizing the scientific environment in and around students' homes. This can include taking nature walks in their neighborhoods, playing science games, and solving science problems in the kitchen or other areas of the house. When children are interested in a particular animal (for example, orca whales or grizzly bears) or hobby (such as race cars or dancing), books and games can provide a world of entertainment and learning.

5. *Decision making* diversifies authority about how things happen in the science classroom to a variety of groups, including teachers, families, and administrators. The main role of each group is to listen and learn from one another without debating or feeling that there is only *one* right answer. Having many diverse perspectives related to school issues or school change can make an educational environment stronger and more successful. To enhance science at the school, you could invite local scientists or science professors to participate as part of a decision-making group.

6. *Community connections* include ways to identify and integrate community resources and services in science activities. Communication in this area includes home and community, school and community, or home, school, and community partnerships. Businesses, museums, health and social service agencies, and other community groups have resources and expertise to strengthen school science programs. For example, a local museum may provide outreach activities in which their museum educators visit the school to enhance students' understanding of a local river environment or mountain habitat. A business may provide equipment and other resources to enhance students' understanding of force and motion.

Building School–Home Partnerships

A disconnect between the home and school environment can create challenges, particularly for children from culturally and linguistically diverse backgrounds. Specifically, although many parents are interested in helping their children in the area of science, many do not feel they have the academic grounding in science needed to support their children's learning. Others may find an open-ended, inquiry-based approach so different from their own textbook-based experiences they are not sure how to help their students. Providing parents with guidance on how to use an inquiry-based approach to science, as well as providing activity suggestions for the home environment, will support the building of a strong home–school partnership in science. This type of overt scaffolding of home–school connections lets parents and families know they are welcome, and acknowledges the funds of knowledge they bring to your school.

Parent Science Nights

One highly successful way to support parents in creating inquiry-based experiences at home is to model just how easily they can be done during a parent science night. Work with your principal to schedule an evening at the school site, and invite all parents to come and learn more about how they can help their child develop their investigative skills at home. Identify other faculty members who may want to participate, and send flyers home well in advance to spread the word about this free enrichment opportunity.

The evening can work many ways. One successful model is to recruit fellow teachers willing to demonstrate easy science activities that can be replicated at home. Paraprofessionals, community members, preservice teachers from local universities, and families with a love of science can also man the activity stations in a series of several breakout sessions. Some helpful hints are as follows:

- Before the session, prepare the areas in which the activities will take place by hanging student work and, in particular, those examples that reflect your efforts in culturally relevant instruction. Photos of students engaged in science activities will attract family members' attention.
- Begin the evening with a general session that provides parents with overarching information on the importance of science learning and how to foster this love of investigation at home. Keep this discussion light and engaging, and tap into cultural touchstones your students have shared with you through some of the methods we have discussed in this book. This will let family members know that you recognize and value all they offer.
- Allow family members to roam the school and visit the different classrooms in which model activities are set up for them to take part. Ensure there are materials available so that multiple family members can participate in the science activities.
- Provide a place for younger children who do not participate in the family science activities.
- Provide transportation for families who need it.
- Provide translators and translate key materials into the native languages of families who attend.
- Provide snacks or other healthy refreshments.
- Send home photocopies of the activity steps and a summary of the key points of the evening. Use pictures along with verbal descriptions for those who are less English proficient.
- Provide a list of science activities that families can do together at home.

Even if you cannot do all these things, doing as many as you can will make your efforts that much more representative of your commitment to developing cultural relevance in your science program.

Integrating Science into Back-to-School Night and Open House Events

Each year, teachers invite families to school as part of an open house event or a back-to-school night. These sessions are usually informal meetings that take place in the late afternoon or evening, during which teachers and students showcase their work, projects, and other activities. These types of events are ideal for highlighting science content. In addition, you and your students can promote science by featuring pictures of them "in action," such as working in cooperative groups or observing habitats in the schoolyard. You might want to create a PowerPoint presentation that is played continuously, or you might skip technology altogether and create a collage with your students to highlight classroom science events. Whatever way you decide to highlight science, make sure that students are included in the planning and implementation of the activity. When planning these events, remember that some families do not have transportation and childcare. Thus, you want to be sure not to attribute a lack of family attendance to some type of deficit view (for example, your students' families do not *care* enough to come to school). Instead, check to see whether your school can provide transportation, snacks, childcare, and/or translators to encourage greater family participation. Know, too, that those who do show up may have little experience with such events; thus, they may hesitate to ask questions, but this does not mean they are not interested!

Student-Led Conferences

Student-led conferences differ from the traditional teacher-led conferences in that you and your students organize the conference together as a team. With student-led conferences, students take a major role in informing their parents about their achievements, interests, and assignments. Students take the initiative to showcase their work and progress during this time. The entire preparation for the conference empowers students to take an integral role in their own learning and to share information with their families about their performance in a less stressful format.

During traditional parent–teacher conferences, teachers do most of the talking and students are not involved in the process. With student-led conferences, the role of students is to help plan the conference, make decisions about the work they would like to show their families, and make statements about their own learning and challenges they have encountered. Your role during this conference is to listen, encourage, support, and answer questions. It is imperative that you and your students notify families in advance about the

TABLE 6.1   Student-Led Conference Science Activities

Sample Science Activity	Time
Interactive family activity, such as making careful observations and recording information about water and air	10 minutes
Interactive family activity, such as participating in a reader's theater related to a science topic	10 minutes
Students' showcase of their work in the form of portfolios, a PowerPoint presentation, or other delivery method	10 minutes
Face-to-face conversation among you, the family, and your student, analyzing the activities and your student's performance at school	10 minutes

conference structure and how their children will be involved. The parent's role is to listen, ask questions, and participate in activities. When students take the lead in the conference, they are empowered to discuss their own learning and can discuss things in their native language, if necessary.

Student-led conferences can be organized in a variety of formats in an effort to include the student, teacher, and family members. A popular student-led conference model includes 40 minutes of participation for each family. The entire conference is led by the students, and facilitated by you and the parents. It should be noted that schools and teachers do not have to appropriate extra funding for these conferences, because the cost of the conference remains the same. Table 6.1 outlines sample activities and time frames associated with science tasks.

Science Inquiry Packs and Science Backpacks

Even though we know inquiry-based science isn't dependent on a set of expensive materials, many families don't have all the materials to conduct learning activities with their children. Creating science inquiry packs that families can check out for use at home can support them in leading science activities with their children. Making sure that each pack has a handout, with visuals, that explains how the activity can be replicated with household items will ensure that science learning will continue long after the pack has been returned. Handouts should be created in multiple languages when necessary.

Inquiry packs can take a variety of forms, depending on the amount of resources available to the teacher. The packs themselves can be purchased very inexpensively at a discount store, or free backpacks might be obtained from the school's unclaimed lost-and-found collection from the previous year or from local thrift stores. The objects inside can be collections of things picked up at garage sales, purchased at discount stores for a few dollars, or may be simply a repackaging of things already in the classroom. A bird kit could include feathers, birdseed, books about local birds from the school library, and well-cleaned egg shells. Another kit could consist of a large magnet and different objects that may or may not be magnetic. Whatever the materials, the key is to put simple directions (in families' native languages) in the pack regarding the types of things to do with the kit. Modeling the use of the kit with younger children prior to sending it home with them can also support its use by turning students into teachers.

You and your school can be proactive and provide a variety of interactive homework assignments that come in ready-to-learn packages, such as backpack science kits. These kits can be part of the science inquiry packs. Companies or retail stores will often donate backpacks to schools or teachers if they indicate that there is a need for them. When participating in backpack science, students take home a backpack that is full of science-related literature and activities that focus on a particular science content area. The activities should be organized so that the whole family can participate when possible. The purpose of backpack science activities is to provide a variety of resources and materials that families may not have at home, and to encourage families and teachers to work together as educational partners.

You can communicate the district science content standards in the backpack materials and include a letter to families that explains the purpose of the backpacks, the activities that should be completed, and any other expectations or directions. (Translate the letters into other languages when appropriate.) Note the information presented Example 6.1. The information is concise and briefly discusses the backpack science activities.

EXAMPLE 6.1 Backpack Homework Assignment

Dear Families,

This month we will begin a new science unit! We will be learning about different animals and where they live. We will focus on science processes such as observing, measuring, and communicating.

I will be sending home science backpacks during the next month that will help you and your child extend this learning at home. There are several books that go along with the science activities. Enjoy reading them together. This should be a fun learning experience for the whole family.

Please contact me if you would like more information.

Ms. Gonzalez

Connecting Science with Students' Lives and Communities

Several times throughout the school year, good teachers make an extra effort to learn about science in their students' lives outside of school. One way to do this is to seek information from students and their families throughout the year as part of an interactive homework assignment.

As students and their families complete the assignment, you should complete the same assignment and provide your answers to students and families. This is a reciprocal approach during which all educational partners share information. It is not one-sided, like traditional family assignments; instead, interactive homework assignments help families and students connect science at home with science at school, and help you learn more about your students (and vice versa). The following are some sample survey prompts:

- Describe or draw anything that you think relates to science in your home.
- Describe or draw animals and pets in your home or neighborhood.
- Describe or draw any favorite collections that you have at home or collections you would like to have.
- Describe or draw your favorite family events.
- Describe or draw your favorite music, books, or games that relate to science around your home or neighborhood.
- Describe or draw the type of plants and trees growing around your home or neighborhood.

It is best if these prompts are sent home throughout the school year to provide information for you, your students, and their families. Note that students should have the opportunity to draw or write their answers to the questions so that the assignment becomes a specific science task rather than a measure of their writing ability. Even more interesting is to provide cameras for students to take home and to photograph areas of their home or neighborhood that relates to science in their lives. After each assignment, students can create class books to show various forms of science in their home and neighborhood. This lets you know what students consider science to be. When done throughout the school year, it allows you and your students to track their science growth and development.

This type of activity further encourages family communication and interactions that examine science at home. It is important for students and families to see science as something that happens in their own homes, in their own neighborhoods, and on a daily basis. Science is not just something that happens at school. When interactive homework is assigned, the activities should be clearly written and in multiple languages if appropriate.

Daily Science Learning Calendar

Developmental Approaches in Science, Health, and Technology (DASH), a program that originated at the University of Hawaii, highlights the importance of implementing a daily learning calendar at school that can be extended to include families and the community. A daily learning calendar can be implemented in kindergarten and can continue for many years. The purpose of the learning calendar is to have students keep a historical record of classroom, community, and world events related to science and other subject areas.

TABLE 6.2 Science Jobs and Sample Tasks

Science Jobs	Sample Tasks
Astronomers	• Record and draw the moon phase • Record and graph the moon rise/moon set • Record and graph sunrise/sunset
Meteorologists	• Record inside and outside temperature • Test and record wind direction and speed using a windsock • Record precipitation using a class rain gauge • Record current and predict future weather conditions
News reporters	• Record international, national, state, and local current events related to science and the environment • Record and draw classroom events
Environmentalists	• Monitor and maintain the recycling center • Monitor and maintain compost • Monitor and maintain classroom areas
Botanists	• Monitor and maintain the classroom plants • Report and draw any changes to classroom plants each week
Zoologists	• Monitor, feed, and maintain the classroom pets and their habitats • Provide a weekly zoologist report based on animal behaviors, sleeping patterns, food consumption, and so forth

One way to organize the learning calendar is to divide students into groups. Each student group is responsible for reporting specific information and recording it on the learning calendar each day for an entire week. Each week, the jobs can change. Table 6.2 shows sample science jobs and tasks; however, you may want to have students determine their own tasks that go with each job.

In upper elementary grades or in middle school, students can determine specific expert groups needed to complete information on the learning calendar. After the information is recorded over time, students can create a chart or graph to identify and describe patterns and anomalies over a period of 20 or 30 days related to their given tasks.

This activity benefits a variety of students, particularly students from non-English backgrounds, because it allows them to

- Work cooperatively in groups to investigate real scientific phenomena
- Use drawings and graphs to record their findings
- Use scientific language that will enhance their use of science vocabulary
- Describe in their own words (or their own language, if appropriate) what they observe related to the tasks they are given to accomplish.

Incorporating Multicultural and Culturally Relevant Materials

When choosing curriculum materials in the form of textbooks, DVDs, computer games, literature, and magazines, consider seeking resources that highlight different races, cultures, and family structures. Look for materials that show children who look different from their parents, children who live with one parent, or children who live with two dads or two moms. In addition, have children provide their own drawings, writings, and interpretations about their families and their families' experiences with science outside the classroom. Consider inviting diverse role models and scientists in the community to visit the classroom or to communicate with students via e-mail or Skype.

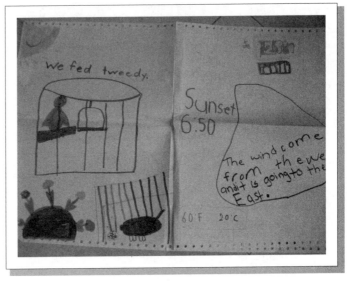

Learning calendar example from second-grade students.

Optional Field Trips

Sometimes there are field trips that simply cannot be fit into the school calendar, either for budgetary reasons or simply because other events take precedence. One way to take part in a field trip that might otherwise be impossible, as well as to create opportunities to connect with families, is to schedule an optional family field trip. Because these take place outside of school hours, they do require you to spend your own personal time to participate. Many teachers find that by committing a few hours on a given Saturday, for example, they can build positive relationships (affective, social, and cognitive) with students and families that save hours of phone calls and note writing throughout the year.

Remember to take lots of photos when you take your field trip so that students can share what they gained from the experience.

To put together a family community field trip, select a location that is easy for parents to reach either through public transportation or straightforward directions. It is also important to select a place that is either free or inexpensive, to ensure maximum participation. Send a note home several weeks in advance that explains that the trip is to be a family field trip that you will be leading, but that all children must arrive with a family member or designated friend. This may even be a classmate whose parent offers to bring both children along if a parent cannot be present. Be sure to indicate in your note that, although this field trip is not required, you hope students and their families will be able to attend.

For the first two hours, facilitate some science activities. After you bid goodbye, however, let students and families know that they are welcome to stay and continue to explore the location. Providing some additional activities, such as an open-ended scavenger hunt or a list of three fun things to see, can help support parents in taking the lead in sharing science with their children in a confident manner. Provide time the following Monday for students to share how they and their family felt about the experience. An optional field trip is likely to be an enriching experience for both students and families alike.

Conducting Home Visits

Teachers and students often live in different communities, and most teachers do not know the families of the students they teach. For teachers, home visits bring greater awareness, understanding, and respect for the student and his or her family. For the families, home visits provide a way for them to get to know their child's teacher, ask questions, and seek information about school events. Moll et al. (1990) encourage teachers to participate in home visits or field studies, particularly as they relate to students from non-English language backgrounds.

During home visits, you are the learner as you attempt to understand the life that students live outside of school. Thus, it is wise to inquire into the cultural backgrounds of students before the home visit to ensure positive interactions between students and their families. For example, if students and their families always leave their shoes outside the door for cultural or religious reasons, then you should be aware of this and do the same.

When you conduct a home visit, families are also able to learn more about you and your expectations for their child's success in science and other subjects. Home visits often open the door for enhanced communication and connections between learning at school and learning at home. The scope of home visits establishes opportunities for more personal contact between you and your students' families outside the school, creates improved conditions in the process of educating children, and supports parents' engagement in their children's education. By looking for the knowledge and strengths of the families, the educational potential of students' households shifts from a deficit view to one that holds possibility, meaning, and educational understanding.

To enhance science at school and home, bring a variety of science objects or activities in which the whole family can participate during the home visit. These interactive science activities can serve as an "ice breaker" for when you first arrive at the home and, in turn, become shared experiences between you, your student, and their family. Vadeboncoeur (2006) has identified five features that influence contexts of learning outside formal classrooms (in other words, informal learning) that relate to planning home visits:

1. *Location:* Where the learning takes place
2. *Relationships:* Who interacts and how in relation to one another
3. *Content:* The type of information and activities that occur
4. *Pedagogy:* How learning takes place
5. *Assessment:* How informal learning is assessed or measured

Using these elements when planning home visits allows you to focus on one or more of these areas to determine how informal learning is centered in students' homes, neighborhoods, and communities. During home visits, students' homes serve as the location for your informal learning, the relationship between you and the family is a learning tool, the content and pedagogy are open depending on the type of activity that you bring with you, and an assessment takes place informally based on the interactions among you, your students, and their families.

Home visits promote personal contact between teachers and students' families in a comfortable environment, create better communication about connecting home life with school life, and support parents' engagement in their children's education (Cox-Petersen, 2010). A culturally relevant science classroom can be enhanced when teachers visit students' homes and interact with the entire family. Patchen et al. (2008) found the following common themes across six different case studies of teachers who conducted home visits.

Common Themes of Teachers Who Conducted Home Visits

1. Teachers expressed professional growth in the area of cultural awareness and appreciation for diverse family beliefs and structures.
2. Teachers gained confidence in their ability to connect with families outside the school.
3. Teachers reported that families were open and expressed their appreciation of the visit.
4. Teachers reported that the parents they visited communicated more frequently after the home visits.
5. Multiple families from different cultural backgrounds demonstrated a willingness to open their homes and meet with teachers.
6. Families demonstrated a strong work ethic and wanted to assist in their child's educational endeavors.

Working Together

When families and teachers work together to communicate strategies, ideas, and expectations, science understanding and achievement are enhanced. This type of reciprocal involvement can be integrated into all curriculum areas, particularly science. More student- and family-active approaches such as home visits and student-led conferences give you the opportunity to learn more about your students and their families as they participate in and learn more about school expectations. In addition, you gain powerful information about your students' families, their beliefs, and interests that will enhance science learning and home–school science connections.

. . . .

95

CASE STUDY   Family Science Night

This was Miss Asir's favorite part of family science night:

"How many of you do science activities with your children at home?" she asked a class-room of first-grade parents and caregivers. They all looked sheepishly from one to another while fewer than 10 people raised their hands. Miss Asir projected an image of a family in the produce aisle of a grocery store on the screen at the front of the room.

"How many of you buy fruits and vegetables with your children?" Almost everyone raised their hand.

"Fruits and vegetables are plants. You're doing botany!" she exclaimed.

Miss Asir then projected a photo of a mother reading the instruction labels on a bottle of cough syrup.

"How many of you are in charge of scraped knees and colds in your family?" she asked. Again, nearly every hand was raised.

"Every time you clean a scrape to prevent infection or choose the right dose of medicine, you are learning and teaching about health!"

Next came a photo of baking a cake.

"Do your children ever help you cook? Have they learned that sugar and salt are not interchangeable in a recipe?" At that, more hands were raised and a little laughter came from the back of the room.

"Believe it or not, mixing ingredients to make a cake is a type of chemistry."

Last came an image of a child feeding a goldfish with a family member looking on.

"How many of you have had to explain that a pet fish doesn't need the whole canister of food in one day?" At this point came more laughter, and chatting with neighbors about similar experiences.

"Knowing about animals and their basic needs is basic zoology!"

Miss Asir then asked, "How many of you do science activities at home with your children?" She was pleased to see every hand raised. The change in the level of confidence was apparent. Family members now realized they were already successfully sharing science with their children. This confidence made them eager to learn even more activities they could try with their children.

Miss Asir then transitioned the group to the evening's activities.

"What we are going to do tonight is learn even more ways you can make science a bigger part of your child's life using things you have lying around the house. We're going to start by investigating a basic chicken egg to learn more about the life cycle of birds. Come and work at any one of the stations we've set up."

Parents excitedly moved to the learning stations. They quickly picked up the handouts that reviewed what was discussed that night, before diving into the hands-on experience. One mother pulled Miss Asir aside and asked when the next science night was scheduled. She couldn't wait to learn more.

(Continued)

Reflecting on the Case

1. What characteristics of culturally relevant instruction did Miss Asir incorporate into her talk with students' parents?

2. How did Miss Asir include families and make them feel more comfortable with the idea about doing science at home and school?

3. How could Miss Asir incorporate funds of knowledge, or each family's strengths and experiences, into the next family science night?

• Book Study Questions •

1. Which type of family involvement do you focus on most in your classroom (based on Epstein's six types)?

2. Which type of family involvement do you think could be improved most?

3. How would you plan and implement home visits with each of your students' families? Name some advantages and challenges.

4. What strengths do students and families bring to your classroom and science instruction?

5. What might you include in a science backpack that would go home with students so that they and their families can engage in science more at home?

6. What type of family science night would work best at your school or in your classroom?

• References and Suggested Readings •

Aikenhead, G. S., & Jegede, O. J. (1999). Cross-cultural science education: A cognitive explanation of a cultural phenomenon. *Journal of Research in Science Teaching, 36,* 269–287.

Barton, A. C., Drake, C., Perez, J. G., St. Louis, K., & George, M. (2004). Ecologies of parental engagement in urban education. *Educational Researcher, 33,* 3–12.

Cox-Petersen, A. (2010). *Educational partnerships: Connecting schools, families, and the community.* Los Angeles, CA: Sage.

Delgado-Gaitan, C. (2004). *Involving Latino families in schools: Raising student achievement through home-school partnerships.* Thousand Oaks, CA: Corwin.

Epstein, J. L. (2001). *School, family, and community partnerships: Preparing educators and improving schools.* Boulder, CO: Westview Press.

Epstein, J. E., & Sanders, M. G. (1998). What we learn from international studies of school-family-community partnerships. *Childhood Education, 74*(6), 392–394.

Lezotte, L. (1997). *Learning for all.* Okemos, MI: Effective School Products.

Moll, L. C., Velez-Ibanez, C., Greenberg, J., & Rivera, C. (1990). *Community knowledge and classroom practice: Combining resources for literacy instruction.* Arlington, VA: Development Associates.

Patchen, T. , Cox-Petersen, A., Ambrose, K., DeVore, A., & Koenings, N. (2008, March). Teachers engaging in informal learning experiences within student' homes. Paper presented at the annual meeting of the American Educational Research Association, New York.

Vadeboncoeur, J. A. (2006). Engaging young people: Learning in informal contexts. *Review of Research in Education, 30,* 239–278.

Keeping Current and Assessing Resources

• Prior Knowledge and Beliefs Organizer •

- Describe the strengths and assets that students and families have that will assist you in teaching science.

- Describe resources (human resources, institutions, community services, and so forth) in your community that can enhance science learning for your students.

Consider your responses to the questions above as you read this chapter and take note of the strengths of the families within your school's community and the wealth of resources available to enhance science teaching and learning.

In this final chapter, we will review some of the culturally relevant ways to encourage science learning for all students by implementing explicit instructional strategies, assessing resources to assist instruction, seeking funding from outside agencies, adhering to policies and procedures, incorporating technology, and tying all the pieces together to provide robust science learning for all students.

The eight explicit strategies encourage you to provide better access to science for all students that will result in a community of science learners today and beyond. To review, consider the following while planning and implementing science lessons:

1. *Inquiry-based instruction:* Engaging students in science experiments, collecting and examining data, and asking authentic questions

2. *Diversifying seating and grouping*: Establishing opportunities for students to work individually, in dyads, and cooperatively in small groups

3. *Connecting students' lives at home:* Linking science practices in the classroom with students' home lives and everyday experiences; reconceptualizing *home*work

4. *Creating a shared learning environment:* Shifting authority so that students take more responsibility in science activities and their own learning

5. *Redistributing authority and redefining classroom responsibilities:* Redesigning and redistributing classroom practices so that students and teachers share in decision making about content and activities

Students participate in a United Nations Day Celebration.

6. *Encouraging real, active, and engaged conversations:* Building on students' knowledge and experiences in the development of meaningful science conversations

7. *Creating a safe environment:* Ensuring student and teacher responses are highly valued and listened to

8. *Developing students' capacity to think and act independently:* Scaffolding students' understanding of science through activities that build self-confidence, develop competence, and motivate learning in science

Assessing Resources

It is important for you, your students, and their families to know about the various resources and opportunities available in the community. One way to do this is to have students inquire and investigate the different programs, materials, and resources around them. They can report on the various nature areas, ecosystems, museums, libraries, or other places that could supplement their science learning. When students take an active role in locating these resources, they will be more motivated to pursue activities that relate to them. Some suggested community resources that students may investigate include a

- Science center
- Aquarium

- Public library
- Local park
- School garden
- County landfill
- Water treatment plant

In addition to specific places that serve as community resources, there are a variety of ways that you, your school, and your students can collaborate with the community. Consider ways to include families and communities at every step. Here are some questions to get you started:

- Is there a local business that might be willing to display student work?
- Can a fun science activity be turned into a family science night?
- Are there college students majoring in science or engineering who would partner with you to build something or to conduct a science experiment?

The most effective science curriculum includes ties to the community and families. Incorporating this element is especially helpful in bringing diverse students and families together for shared science events.

Planning and Preparation for Science

Planning and preparation is an important component to successful science instruction. Advanced preparation can be even more critical as you strive to procure needed materials, prepare for differentiated instruction, and anticipate concepts that will need special attention.

Inquiry-based instruction is most effective when sufficient time is provided for students to direct their own learning. It is important to set aside time for students who are culturally and linguistically diverse to explore concepts at their own pace and to create a timeline that provides the opportunity for needed remediation. In addition, develop vocabulary during experiences, and allow students to make connections between new knowledge and labels, and their prior knowledge.

District Policies and Regulations

All schools and districts have regulations that are in place for student and teacher safety. Be sure to check on any restrictions before moving forward with a new approach to the curriculum. Although walking to the local park is a great way to teach your students about plant life cycles, without appropriate parental permission, the field trip goes from a great learning experience to grounds for faculty discipline. There's no need to be constrained by all district regulations, however. A school with a "no live animals" policy may be easily convinced that a brief visit by a snake or parakeet will be a great way for students to learn about animal adaptations by writing a well-thought-out proposal and citing other schools that are using a similar model.

Space Usage

Thinking creatively about space is helpful when pushing forward any new science project. Inquiry-based science requires space to store materials and connections with the outdoors, and opportunities for students to work in small groups. You may want to explore the schoolyard to determine whether there are spaces for a native garden, or explore the community to highlight natural areas that may be within walking distance of the school. It can be difficult to store the hands-on materials at the center of an inquiry-based science program. Search the school grounds for unused storage spaces or cabinets in workrooms, or propose erecting an inexpensive storage cabinet or shed.

Instructional Methods

A popular way to ensure all students' needs are met is to enact *differentiated instruction* during science instruction. Differentiated instruction includes a lesson taught for a large group of students while focusing on meeting the needs of each child. With roots in gifted education and special education, content and instructional strategies can be modified so that every child can succeed. For example, if the content in a fourth-grade classroom focuses on the formation of rocks, the teacher can determine multiple instructional strategies to help students understand this concept while considering various learning styles:

- Provide clay and other materials, and have students manipulate the clay to simulate the formation of different types of rocks: igneous, metamorphic, and sedimentary

- Show students a video of the creation of a formation of rocks while featuring different rock formations

- Encourage groups of students to create a script and act out the creation of rocks

Provide lots of materials for kids to explore and inquire.

While differentiating instruction, all methods that you provide for students have equal value. In addition, students can choose in which activity or activities they would like to engage to understand science concepts or to develop scientific skills.

Providing a Rationale for "Messy Science"

As you plan your curriculum, it is important to articulate the instructional methods you will use and record them in your plans. Sometimes administrators walk into classrooms in the throes of inquiry-based science that may include heated discussion, exuberant voices explaining a discovery, or a dirty, messy hands-on exploration. Without the proper context, these experiences are often misunderstood and not seen for the effective instructional techniques they are. Articulating in a planning book the active, experiential methods you'll be using (and any differentiated instruction) connected to science standards will assure administrators, parents, and fellow teachers that your inquiry-based, student-centered approaches are valid.

Integration of Technology

The appropriate use of technology is critical to supporting all students in the 21st century. In addition, technology is a tool that can help culturally and linguistically diverse students build content knowledge and experiences by interacting with other students or by engaging in scientific reading and activities online. In addition, there are a variety of materials that can enhance science instruction:

- *Video flip cameras and digital cameras* enhance observational skills and document scientific evidence in a variety of settings.
- *Science probes* gather a variety of data for science activities and experiments, such as light and temperature recorders, motion and sound sensors, and heart rate monitors.
- *Microscopes for computers* can be projected on a screen for the entire class to participate in discussing, observing, and analyzing specimens.

Online Partnerships

Online partnerships allow students and teachers to exchange information around the world in a matter of seconds. One project, the GLOBE Program, is a hands-on environmental science and educational endeavor that recruits an international network of students in elementary, middle, and high schools who are studying environmental issues. Groups of students from all over the globe make environmental measurements and share environmental data with the international environmental science community.

The Science Controversies On-line: Partnerships in Education (SCOPE) Project was developed by the University of California at Berkeley, University of Washington, and the American Association for the Advancement of Science. This group features an online knowledge network community wherein scientists, educators, and students can learn more science research and controversies related to processes, procedures, and outcomes.

The Global SchoolNet Foundation connects students and teachers throughout the world to provide global perspective related to issues in schools and classrooms. Students investigate collaboratively community, culture, and public science issues that will assist them in becoming responsible and respectful world citizens. The program provides a variety of materials and resources for teachers, including special offers from Global School-Net funders and partners.

Webquests

Webquests are one way to challenge students to explore a single topic or concept in greater depth using the Internet as a resource. Webquests provide structure to support students in their exploration of online resources while retaining the element of student-directed learning. Because webquests can be created using any complexity of webpage, they can be specially tailored to the needs of ELLs and to individual levels of literacy.

Citizen Science

There are a number of national projects focused on tapping into students as collectors of environmental data. As Web-based experiences, students in any school can participate. Because of their national and international emphasis, they highlight for students that science is done by all types of people around the world. For culturally and linguistically diverse students, they can see themselves more globally represented in science careers. Highlighting this diversity of science and scientists is important to providing role models and various scientific perspectives. For all students, citizen science projects offer students a view of science outside the classroom.

Social Networking Sites

For many of us, social networking sites provide an opportunity to connect more regularly with our circle of friends, acquaintances, family, and colleagues on life events. These can also be helpful in connecting with resources to support classroom instruction. A quick posting might request postcards that highlight local wildlife, reports of temperatures from north to south, and even sand samples from coast to coast. Social networking sites include the popular Facebook and Twitter.

Funding Resources

Parent Support

Many schools and districts have parent organizations focused on supporting the school curriculum and providing needed funds for special projects. By connecting with the principal or district office, you can identify opportunities for appropriately approaching parent support groups. Some may have small grant opportunities in place; others may look to the district office for guidance in funding programs. Also, there are a variety of organizations and corporations that provide grant money for teachers, and many grants focus on science-related activities and projects.

Community Donations

There is a wealth of resources in your own community to support science instruction for culturally and linguistically diverse students. Many educators know that objects and hands-on experiences are the most effective in reaching culturally and linguistically diverse students. However, many don't realize that they can get a lot of these resources right inside their own community. A local farmers market may be willing to donate some produce for a unit on nutrition. A local home improvement shop may be willing to donate samples of landscaping rocks for geology studies. A local nursery may be interested in providing plants for a school garden or a tree to commemorate a special event such as Earth Day or Arbor Day.

Grant Funding

A *grant* is a written agreement that is usually attached to funding for a particular program or project. *Requests for proposals* (RFPs) are developed and advertised by state or federal government agencies, private foundations, or corporations. RFPs usually target a specific type of program for which an agency or corporation is interested in providing funding. Many grants are competitive, but they offer educators or organizations various sums of money to implement an innovative project. Some grants fund classroom materials, other grants support districtwide initiates, and yet other grants support professional development opportunities for teachers. There are specific guidelines that you must follow when writing a grant proposal. Many government agencies, foundations, and corporations provide strategies and examples to assist educators in writing grant proposals.

There are a number of grant opportunities for educators that range from small materials grants to larger amounts for projects linked to systemic change. Because many educational grants are state or county specific, an exhaustive list is beyond the scope of this publication. However, a simple Internet search or discussion with your district office can easily identify a number of offerings to explore.

Making the Request for Grant Funding   Whoever you approach for support, a well-organized plan and thoughtful approach is the key to any successful request. Here are a few do's and don'ts:

DO have a well-organized plan.

DON'T ask for money without being able to articulate clearly how it will be used.

DO highlight your successes and how the additional funds will help you accomplish additional goals.

DON'T focus only on the negative. Funders want to have confidence you can succeed with the gift they provide.

DO base your request on research, evidence, and the best interests of your students.

DON'T make your need personal.

DO be realistic in your expectations.

DON'T make unlikely promises. For example, $200 in science materials is unlikely to raise student test scores immediately for the entire third grade.

DO highlight how the unique needs of your students, such as those who may have disabilities or may be culturally and linguistically diverse, can be met by this funding.

DON'T assume student attributes are the sole reason your proposal should be supported.

DO double-check the details of your proposal, request letter, or introductory e-mail.

DON'T let typos, incorrectly added figures, or outdated research slip past you.

EXAMPLE 7.1   Incorrect Approach to Obtaining Grant Funding

Every year there are more and more budget cuts. Right now I have to spend my own money just to buy the science supplies we need for students to learn anything. I just can't afford to do this anymore. In fact, our school is doing so poorly in science—almost failing state tests—without these materials I just don't think my students can succeed. As English language learners, they need these special services and no one seems to understand that.

EXAMPLE 7.2 A Better Approach to Obtaining Grant Funding

National test scores indicate that many students are struggling with science. Here at Oak Street Elementary we are experiencing similar difficulties. In fact, our students performed at the lowest tier on the most recent state assessment, despite several intervention strategies we've used during the past two years. One very specific hurdle we have not been able to overcome is a lack of quality materials. Research tells us that hands-on experiences are critical for helping English language learners (Watson & Houtz, 2002), which make up the majority of our school population. Unfortunately, we don't have the funds to provide quality materials consistently. Support from your organization would help us add this final element to our plan to provide a valued and cohesive science program for all students.

Writing a Grant Proposal   The very first thing you should do before you begin writing a grant proposal is to read all the requirements and expectations that the grant specifies. RFPs usually state the goals of the grant and on what the project should focus, such as a particular subject area or science topic. After you have read the requirements, determine whether it is a project that fits your needs, grade level, and facilities available at your school site.

Read the requirements of the grant carefully to make sure you have addressed every area when creating a draft of your grant proposal. It is helpful to use a highlighter to mark what is required, who is involved, and the instructions for formatting the proposal. Usually, the granting agency will require that you reveal your goals, objective, summary of the project, a timeline of events, responsible parties, and a budget. After you have written your grant and have had several of your colleagues proof it, determine how and when to submit your proposal. Many grants feature online submission forms; other grant submissions require a specific number of copies mailed to specified addresses.

- *Goals* include overarching long-range outcomes.
- *Objectives* include short-term, measurable outcomes to help meet your goals.
- *A summary of the project* includes a brief description of the activities and innovative ideas.
- *A timeline of events* usually includes a list of activities, the person or people

SIDEBAR 7.1
Align Your Objectives to Your Proposal

Make sure that your outcomes stated in your goals and your objectives align with the activities listed in your project description, your timeline, and your budget. Be specific about your plans when describing your project and provide examples when possible. For some grants, you can include charts or bullet points to highlight important information or project tasks.

who will carry out the activities, and the date when the activities will be implemented.

- *A budget* includes a list of all expenses associated with the project and a description or justification for them.

Grants Available to Schools and Teachers

General grant information websites, and grants related to science education and teacher recognition/professional development are presented in this section. The list includes grants available for teachers from organizations and corporations. Most government-sponsored grants change from year to year. You can access the most current grant-funding opportunities on their respective websites.

General Grants: Information and Resources

- Teachers Network: Teacher Grants   *www.teachersnetwork.org/grants/*
  This site provides lesson plans and unit plans, and lists a variety of granting agencies and information. The grant information is organized by subject area, such as science, social studies, or mathematics. The site also provides a list of steps for writing grant proposals.

- The Science House   *www.science-house.org/teacher/grants/index.html*
  This site provides tips for writing grants and obtaining science resources.

- Grants Alert   *www.grantsalert.com/gsft.cfm*
  The Grants Alert website offers information related to current grant requests. This site provides teachers with access and information related to funding opportunities.

Grants Related to Science Education

- Toyota Tapestry Grants   *www.nsta.org/pd/tapestry/*
  Teachers can apply for a variety of awards and grants that include students, families, and the community. These competitive grants are awarded yearly by Toyota Motor Sales USA and the National Science Teachers Association. You can view prior awards and websites related to past projects.

- American Institute of Aeronautics and Astronautics Classroom Grant   *www.aiaa. org/content.cfm?pageid=216*
  This grantor provides supplements to existing academic programs. These can include demonstrations kits, science supplies, math and science software, graphing supplies, and similar materials to help integrate science, math, and technology in the classroom.

- Lowe's Toolbox for Education Grant Program   *www.toolboxforeducation.com/*
  Lowe's Charitable and Educational Foundation (or LCEF) is an advocate of

parent–teacher groups to encourage more involvement. This grant program provides money for public school improvement projects for a variety of curriculum areas.

- NASA Educational Grants and Resources *www.nasa.gov/offices/education/about/index.html*
  This site provides a variety of information related to earth and space science, and features resources for teachers and students. It also lists current grant and award opportunities.

Grants to Promote and Recognize Teachers

- The Freida J. Riley Teacher Award *http://nmoe.org/riley/index.htm*
  This annual award recognizes a teacher who affects students profoundly and positively. This teacher traditionally gets recognition for overcoming some type of adversity or for making a considerable sacrifice.

- Foundation Educator Achievement Award *www.aiaa.org/content.cfm?pageid=217*
  The American Institute of Aeronautics and Astronautics pays tribute to seven teachers every two years for their accomplishments with K−12 students. This award goes to teachers who inspire and excite students about math, science, and technology.

- National Teachers Hall of Fame Teacher Recognition *www.nthf.org/teacher.htm*
  This national teacher recognition honors five teachers annually. Candidates include those who have demonstrated commitment and dedication to teaching. Awards also include a scholarship for a student pursuing an education career and a monetary gift for classroom materials.

- Presidential Awards for Excellence in Science and Mathematics Teaching *www.paemst.org/*
  This award is administered by the White House and the National Science Foundation. Teachers must demonstrate their exemplary contributions in their classroom and in their professional community related to math and science. Winners in each state receive a $10,000 classroom award; a trip to Washington, DC, to attend congratulatory events; and additional gifts from sponsors.

- Earthwatch Teacher Fellowships *www.earthwatch.org/aboutus/education/edopp*
  Grants are made available to teachers to participate in one of the many Earthwatch expeditions with top researchers at sites around the world. Past research expeditions have included a study of Australia's forest marsupials, dolphins of Greece, Easter Island cultures, and Alaskan glaciers. Teachers who are awarded fellowships can receive funding that covers their participation in one of the research expeditions, food, accommodations, and onsite travel. Some fellowships also cover travel reimbursement.

CASE STUDY Mrs. Rey and Hands-On Science

Mrs. Rey was really excited about the upcoming geology unit. It was a topic she knew could be taught through many different modalities. This experience would provide an opportunity for some of her students struggling with English fluency to be successful. It was also a chance for some of her kinesthetic learners to be successful. With so many hands-on projects planned, she knew it would also be a truly enjoyable unit for all students, something that would be especially helpful in motivating a few of her students who were starting to get discouraged in other academic areas. Mrs. Rey's class consisted of students from a variety of cultures and with varying levels of English language proficiency. Some were born in the United States whereas others were new arrivals to the country. Differentiated instruction was a critical part of every day for her.

She began by blocking off mandated minutes of science instruction in her plan book for the next six weeks. Knowing what blocks of time she had to work with was going to help her match the right activity with the time allotted. Nothing was worse than students feeling rushed or having to move quickly past a topic when they were still excited to learn more. She reviewed the standards to make sure she was comfortable with the concepts that needed to be addressed, and then she began to get creative.

First, she planned to use their single annual field trip in conjunction with this unit. They had a wonderful natural history museum in their city with a brand-new gem and mineral exhibit. This would be a great way for students to experience specimens that she could never access. She marked it in her plan book halfway through the six-week unit. This would ensure they had a little background for the experience, but it also allowed them to look back on their shared experience as they proceeded through the unit. She knew the exhibit had gems and minerals from around the world. She thought this would be an added benefit—the opportunity for some of her students who were new to America to make connections between the classroom curriculum and their home country.

Mrs. Rey then went to her supply closet and pulled out a storage box with her own personal rock collection. There were sedimentary rocks she had brought back from a recent hike in a nonprotected area. There was lava rock that she got from her mother's front yard (her mother used it as landscape material). Many of the samples came from her local home improvement store, which sold them for landscaping. Her request for five or six individual rocks from their large landscaping bags was something they were more than happy to provide. These samples would be invaluable in providing shared experiences between students and in helping them explore differences in density and texture.

Next she sat down in front of her classroom library. She wanted to pull all the books that were related to geology—both fiction and nonfiction—and have these books displayed around the classroom. She had many students who were struggling readers. Pairing new vocabulary in the books with the hands-on activities would help with comprehension. It might also motivate some of her more reluctant readers.

Last, she made a note to herself to bring in her global jewelry collection. An avid traveler, she made a point to buy a necklace, ring, or bracelet from every place she visited. She had turquoise from Mexico, malachite from Kenya, and jade from Japan. All these pieces were inexpensive, so students would have the opportunity to hold them and wear them, and make connections between the science of geology and cultural stories. This was often a popular activity among students and often prompted them to bring in geology-related mementos from their own countries for class discussion.

Although there was still much to do, it was time for her to leave for the day. She was going to look through some of her DVDs at home and determine whether there were any that might also be helpful to the lesson.

Reflecting on the Case

1. What are the advantages that Mrs. Rey had by planning ahead with a variety of resources?

2. How could students take advantage of online partnerships with other schools to enhance this unit?

3. Use the Internet to investigate different educational grants for which Mrs. Rey might apply to supplement her geology unit.

4. How might Mrs. Rey make this unit culturally relevant and accessible for all students?

Final Comments

This book only begins to provide information, strategies, and insight into teaching science for all students and in a culturally relevant way. First and foremost, students' science ideas and beliefs should be valued. Students begin to figure out how the world works and to notice science in their world (although perhaps not consciously) even before formal schooling takes place. The science classroom is a way to motivate students to *like* science, feel confident about doing science, and integrate science at school with science in their home and community. For the most part, you cannot change the content that is mandated by your state and district. However, what you can change are your instructional strategies, your interactions with students, and the way you empower students to learn science.

We hope that you use this book as a reference when incorporating a variety of instructional models, creating partnerships with families, and assessing students' knowledge of science in multiple ways. All students can learn science and can be competent in science if we add just a few culturally relevant strategies to our daily instruction.

• Book Study Questions •

1. How can you use technology to motivate students to learn more about science?

2. What instructional strategies can you use to provide more culturally relevant experiences for your students?

3. What type of science project can you think of for which you might seek grant funding to make your science lessons more culturally relevant and accessible to all students?

4. How can you work with families more to get them involved in science at school and at home?

5. What is the most important strategy that you will apply to science from all the chapters in this book?

6. What struck you the most about this book and teaching science to your students, particularly students from culturally and linguistically diverse backgrounds?